Praise for

How to Find Selfless Joy in a Me-First World

"*How to Find Selfless Joy in a Me-First World* will challenge you to go deeper in your walk with God. Leslie Vernick has done a masterful job of weaving biblical principles on humility with poignant, real-life illustrations that demonstrate how to be an authentic Christ-follower. The carefully chosen quotations and the discussion questions for each chapter make this an ideal choice for small-group studies and will produce transformational results."

>—CAROL KENT, president of Speak Up Speaker Services, international
>speaker, and author of *Becoming a Woman of Influence*

"Vernick cuts to the chase regarding the two most popular—and most abused—words of our culture: love and self. She capably teaches us that lasting joy or satisfaction never, ever comes independent of our Creator's intimate plans for us. Through her common-sense approach, we are reminded of the very first lesson many of us heard in church: God is love. Without God, there is no love."

>—RONALD T. HABERMAS, PH.D., McGee Professor of Biblical Studies
>and Christian Formation, John Brown University, and author of
>*The Complete Disciple*

"Leslie Vernick's latest book uncovers wisdom that was known to Christians throughout history but has been lost in our contemporary world. She exposes the self-serving, self-boosting advice we receive so constantly from both secular and Christian sources as not only sinful,

but useless. It just doesn't work. Her prescription is the same as Jesus': Die to self, serve others, and discover joy. Paradoxically, this is the only route to joy there is."

—FREDERICA MATHEWES-GREEN, commentator for National Public
   Radio, author, and essayist

"Leslie Vernick has done it again! Insightful and inspiring, practical and prophetic, *How to Find Selfless Joy in a Me-First World* calls Christians to live a life counter to our contemporary self-obsessed culture. If you are serious about being an authentic Christ-follower in the real world, this book is a must-read."

—DR. SAMUEL D. RIMA, author of *Leading from the Inside Out* and
   Rethinking the Successful Church

"*How to Find Selfless Joy in a Me-First World* offers solid truth about the hardest challenges contemporary Christians face. Leslie reminds us, gently but directly, that only God can be God. Read it and be encouraged!"

—BRENDA WAGGONER, licensed counselor and author of *Fairy Tale Faith*

"This is a dangerous book! If you read it, you will discover your hidden (or not-so-hidden) me-first living. Has 'feasting at the table of cheap substitutes' dulled your sense of joy and pleasure? If so, this book will enable you to recapture the greater, more fulfilling joy of knowing the presence of God."

—PHIL MONROE, PSY.D., director, M.A. Counseling Program,
   Biblical Theological Seminary

"We have been taught by the world that joy and happiness come wrapped in the illusions of possessions, titles, and positions in life. In *How to Find Selfless Joy in a Me-First World*, Leslie points us back to the reality that true joy can only be found in God! Through the practical, thought-provoking study included in this book, Leslie challenges us with the knowledge that to find true selfless joy we must strive to know God and be conformed into his image."

—SUE RIMA, director of Women's Ministry for the

Columbia Baptist Conference

How to Find Selfless Joy in a Me-First World

How to Find Selfless Joy in a Me-First World

LESLIE VERNICK

WATERBROOK
PRESS

HOW TO FIND SELFLESS JOY IN A ME-FIRST WORLD
PUBLISHED BY WATERBROOK PRESS
2375 Telstar Drive, Suite 160
Colorado Springs, Colorado 80920
A division of Random House, Inc.

All Scripture quotations, unless otherwise indicated, are taken from the *Holy Bible, New International Version*®. NIV®. Copyright © 1973, 1978, 1984 by International Bible Society. Used by permission of Zondervan Publishing House. All rights reserved. Scripture quotations marked (MSG) are taken from *The Message*. Copyright © by Eugene H. Peterson 1993, 1994, 1995. Used by permission of NavPress Publishing Group. Scripture quotations marked (NASB) are taken from the *New American Standard Bible*®. © Copyright The Lockman Foundation 1960, 1962, 1963, 1968, 1971, 1972, 1973, 1975, 1977, 1995. Used by permission. (www.Lockman.org). Scripture quotations marked (NKJV) are taken from the *New King James Version*. Copyright © 1982 by Thomas Nelson, Inc. Used by permission. All rights reserved.

Details in some anecdotes and stories have been changed to protect the identities of the persons involved.

ISBN 1-57856-398-4

Library of Congress Cataloging-in-Publication Data
Vernick, Leslie.
    How to find selfless joy in a me-first world / Leslie Vernick.— 1st ed.
      p. cm.
    ISBN 1-57856-398-4
    1. Joy—Religious aspects—Christianity. 2. Christian life. I. Title.
    BV4647.J68V47 2003
    248.4—dc21
                        2003006168

Printed in the United States of America
2003—First Edition

10   9   8   7   6   5   4   3   2   1

In loving memory of my mother, Joan.

I'm so thankful that God brought you back into my life

and allowed me the joy of bringing you

to the gates of heaven.

(1933–2003)

Contents

Foreword

I was once asked to write an article for a Christian magazine on the topic of selflessness. After turning in the first draft, I received an e-mail back from the editor. He praised the work but asked that I expand a section addressing the "rewards" of selflessness.

The irony made me laugh. "Okay, I'll be unselfish," the thinking goes, "but if I do that, what's in it for me?"

For the apostle Paul, selflessness was a way of life: "We who are strong ought to bear with the failings of the weak and not to please ourselves. Each of us should please his neighbor for his good, to build him up. For even Christ did not please himself" (Romans 15:1-3).

In fact, Paul took this line of thinking one step further. "Though I am free and belong to no man, *I make myself a slave to everyone,* to win as many as possible" (1 Corinthians 9:19, emphasis added). Because Paul's writings are so familiar to us, it is easy to miss the astonishing depth to which he was willing to descend to put himself completely at others' disposal. Think about it: a slave *to everyone?*

The extreme to which Paul adhered to this selflessness is, in fact, shocking to modern sensibilities. He tells the Romans that he wishes he could cut himself off from salvation if in doing so he could save Israel (Romans 9:3). Paul was fully aware of the horrors of hell—the physical pain, the emotional angst, the spiritual alienation. Yet how many of us could truly say, "If in the twilight of descending to hell I could look over my shoulder and see my unsaved brothers and sisters marching into heaven, I would make that choice"?

Where did Paul get this selflessness? How could a man become so others-oriented, so willing to play the role of a servant? Paul took the words of Jesus—"It is more blessed to give than to receive" (Acts 20:35)—literally and found that they were true. Throughout his letters, Paul is effusive with his thanks and affection for others. Clearly, his service on their behalf brought tremendous joy to his life: "In all my prayers for all of you, I always pray with joy.... It is right for me to feel this way about all of you, since I have you in my heart" (Philippians 1:4,7). Paul's affection for others was real; the enjoyment he derived from serving them and sacrificing on their behalf was tangible and at times intense. "For I wrote you out of great distress and anguish of heart and with many tears, not to grieve you but to let you know the depth of my love for you" (2 Corinthians 2:4). These are not the words of a man who grudgingly serves. These are the words of a man who has found service to be the foundation of the most meaningful life imaginable, fostering an intimacy many of us could only dream about. Ironically, this attitude of selflessness actually creates a fountain of joy that refreshes our faith with meaning and soothes our pain with purpose.

This is the truth that Leslie Vernick captures for us and explores in depth in her very important book *How to Find Selfless Joy in a Me-First World*. The ancients called humility "the queen of the virtues," which makes *Selfless Joy* a queen among books. In a world obsessed with self-fulfillment and self-actualization, Leslie calls us back to biblical truth: We are to live for the glory of God, who calls us to a life of selfless service and even sacrifice. Though it appears that such a life is radically indifferent to our culture's pursuit of "happiness," it is in actuality the most certain path to true biblical joy.

Leslie captures this reality with the title alone, but the body of her book has enough bread for many famished souls. Read this book with an open heart and a repentant spirit. All who make the spiritual correction that Leslie proposes will find themselves filled with joy.

GARY THOMAS
Center for Evangelical Spirituality
www.garythomas.com

Acknowledgments

This book is not my own, and so I owe a debt of gratitude to the men and women of God, both past and present, who have deeply shaped and influenced me. They have experienced a life well lived, and I pray that I, too, will walk in their example.

Committing these ideas and experiences to paper required me to grow in my faith and trust in God. Each page became a battlefield as Satan dogged my mind with accusations of pride, self-centeredness, and selfishness, all of which I imagine I will always struggle with this side of heaven. I am so grateful for my prayer team, who faithfully upheld me while I was writing. They are the unseen part of the body of Christ who function selflessly, serving namelessly and sacrificially for the glory of God and the good of others. They know the joy of a selfless heart in a me-first world.

Thank you to my AWSA (Advanced Writers and Speakers Association) sisters, who also bathed me and my family in prayer. How wonderful to work with a group of women who know what your life is like and offer loving support and encouragement instead of jealous competition. Theresa Cain, my soul sister and dear friend, thank you for your penetrating questions, keen observations, and willingness to get in my face when necessary. I thank God for you.

Georgia Shaffer, Christopher Zang, Glenna Dameron, and my pastor, Howard Lawler: Thank you for your insights and comments as well as giving your valuable time to read through my first draft. I trust you will find your time well spent, as I have gratefully incorporated many of your comments. Marg Hinds, my assistant, thank you for keeping me together and doing all the things I hate to do.

To my husband, Howard, and my children, Ryan and Amanda, I love you. I'm proud to be your wife and mom. Thank you for fanning the flame of the gifts God has given me. Without your support and help, I would be lost.

The people at WaterBrook Press are amazing. You believed in this project and listened to me when I needed to make a shift. I am very grateful. My editor Erin Healy's masterful shuffling and reorganizing helped this book come into greater clarity.

As a Christian counselor, I have had the privilege of sitting with many people who have generously shared their stories with me. Thank you for trusting me. Rest assured that each story is disguised so that your identity is protected.

Last but never least, dearest Lord Jesus, thank you for giving me the highest honor a human being could ever have—to know you and to serve you. May I do so with all my heart, soul, mind, and strength.

How often in our innocence,
    which Jesus calls self-centeredness,
We think that when God blesses me
    the whole world will rejoice to see
    that Jesus is alive in me!

We do not see God's perfect scheme
    to strip us of our dearest dream
Of world-renown and fantasy,
    (whatever level it may be)
    of blessings other people see.

His greatest blessing oft may be
    the blessing of humility:
That never will His words be won
    from others' lips, nor praises come
    from any voice but His alone:
"How blessed you are, My faithful one!"[1]

—from "How Blessed You Are" by L. M. Miles

Introduction

How Happy We Should All Be

When I was a child, I loved the story of Pinocchio, the wooden marionette who longed to become a real boy. If only he were real, he believed, he would be happy. He thought he would find what he craved if he were free to live as he pleased—to eat, sleep, and play whenever he wanted, without anyone telling him what to do. But in his quest for a better life, Pinocchio continually ran into mishaps. He disdained school and was allergic to work. People who loved him tried to influence Pinocchio to choose a different path, but he refused to listen and was easily fooled with promises of fun and fortune.

Many painful lessons later, Pinocchio finally began to grasp that if he wanted to find true happiness, he would need to focus on something besides pleasing himself and having a good time. Pinocchio began to work hard on his school lessons, and he tried to be less self-centered and selfish. But one night, Pinocchio's good friend Lamp-wick enticed him to run away with him to the Land of Toys. Lamp-wick crowed, "I'm going to a real country...the best in the world...it's a wonderful place!" Initially Pinocchio refused, but Lamp-wick persisted, saying, "You'll be sorry!"

Pinocchio struggled with what to do. Should he stay on what looked like the harder path and continue his schooling, or should he take the easier road straight to the Land of Toys? *Wow,* Pinocchio mused, *imagine a place where there is no school, no teachers or books. A place where no one studies or works and every day is like vacation. Sounds wonderful, too good to miss.* Pinocchio's resolve quickly melted, and he eagerly agreed to run away with Lamp-wick. "This is the place for me!" Pinocchio exclaimed. "All countries should be like it. How happy we should all be." And—for a while—that's exactly what it seemed.

Until the day Pinocchio woke up and discovered his ears were twice as big as usual.

When he peered into a basin of water, what Pinocchio saw staring back at him gave him a start. His ears and snout were growing! He was changing, but not into the real boy that he longed to become. He was turning into a donkey, just like the ones harnessed to the wooden cart that towed the boys to the Land of Toys. Pinocchio suddenly understood that he had chosen the wrong path. He realized that he had been foolish to think that living for himself and for pleasure would make him happy. Those things didn't free him or make him happy; they degraded and enslaved him.

Over the years I have observed that many Christians feel just as miserable as Pinocchio, just as sad. For various reasons we are unhappy with ourselves, our marriages, our God, and our lives. Sometimes we struggle to make friends or keep them. Often we feel disappointed when we look in the mirror. Like Pinocchio, we are searching for a way to become more real, to make life more fulfilling, to experience more happiness. We wonder why we do not live the abundant life that Jesus promised. We tell ourselves it's because we suffer from low self-esteem and a poor self-image. If only we felt better about ourselves, had more self-confidence, then—maybe—we'd feel happy.

The world promises us that if we find ourselves, fulfill ourselves, love ourselves, and satisfy ourselves, we will indeed become happy. Daily we're bombarded with slogans that guarantee we would find more satisfaction in life and feel better about ourselves if only we had whiter teeth, a Platinum MasterCard, or a certain type of car. Friends and counselors alike often suggest that we can never be happy in a difficult marriage or content if we are deficient in self-love.

But does living for self ever bring anyone lasting joy or satisfaction? I believe the answer is a resounding no!

When we live to please our passions and allow pride to direct our steps, God tells us we make a very bad choice. (See, for example, Deuteronomy 30:11-20; Isaiah 30; Jeremiah 7:23-34.) We may not become literal donkeys, but we do become disfigured. We grow to be less and less the person God designed us to be. Sin may be fun for a season, and often it seems true that pursuing pleasure and self-centered goals makes people happy. But the truth is, sin degrades the human being; it makes us into something we were never intended to be (Romans 1:28). One has only to watch today's talk-show guests to see how living for pleasure and for self affects a person's mind, heart, and soul—not to mention the havoc it wreaks on one's relationships with others.

The Bible warns us that there is a way that may seem right, but in the end it leads to death (Proverbs 14:12). Pinocchio learned the hard way that he would find lasting happiness only when he stopped being self-centered and started to live for something bigger than finding or pleasing himself. He learned that thinking solely of himself hurt those he loved, and their unhappiness made him sad.

Over time I have learned both personally and professionally that what often seems right to me is contrary to what God teaches. As I have studied God's Word more carefully and taken what he has said to heart, my life has changed. I have found that the gifts of a life well lived and inner happiness are not laced with the bows of self-indulgence, self-fulfillment, self-love, self-esteem, and self-importance; they are more often bound with the cords of self-denial and self-forgetfulness.

Like Pinocchio, I have also come to understand that the virtue of humility, or selflessness, provides a more fertile ground for personal, relational, and spiritual joy than does working toward self-improvement, self-esteem, or self-fulfillment. As Pinocchio eventually discovered, we will only find our true selves and genuine happiness when we learn to live for something beyond pleasing, satisfying, or loving ourselves. Throughout Scripture, God tells us that humankind's greatest joy and deepest satisfaction doesn't come through loving ourselves better but through loving him with our whole heart. He then empowers us to love others unselfishly, which enhances our joy and satisfaction with life.

Lasting happiness only comes as a result of being rightly related to God, to others, and to ourselves. If we are not, life will ultimately feel empty and meaningless. We might enjoy temporary pleasures, like the way we feel after buying some new toy or savoring a tasty meal. But that kind of happiness never lasts long. Soon we find ourselves chasing the next pleasure, the next thrill, the next dream of what we think might bring us more happiness. In our quest, we might accumulate lots of stuff and achieve a fat bank account or job security. We may look great and have plenty of self-confidence. But if we don't know ourselves and know God, if we don't experience being deeply loved and we don't love others back, then we will never be happy or know the blessings of a life well lived. If our relationship with God is superficial, dull, or merely theological, we won't experience the inner joy and deep satisfaction that our souls are designed to enjoy. We might be wealthy or smart or beautiful or powerful, but these things never bring any lasting happiness.

I pray this book will stimulate your hunger and thirst for God while at the same time dulling your appetite for yourself and your own agenda for life.

So come—come to the living water, those of you who are thirsty for a joy-filled soul—and find it in the place you least expect. Find it as a hidden treasure along the dusty and oft-forsaken path of selfless-ness. Ponder the words of Thomas à Kempis who wisely counseled, "For indeed by loving myself amiss, I lost myself...and seeking Thee alone, and purely loving Thee, I have found both myself and Thee."[1]

1

Our Perilous Pursuit of Self

It is vain, O men, that you seek within yourselves
the cure for your miseries. All your insight only leads you
to the knowledge that it is not in yourselves
that you will discover the true and the good.

<small>BLAISE PASCAL</small>

One of the first lessons I learned in my counselor's training is that nothing said is insignificant, especially the opening and the closing words of a session. Jonathan came to see me at his wife's request. She was dissatisfied with their marriage and contacted me after reading my book *How to Act Right When Your Spouse Acts Wrong.* She described her husband as depressed and uninvolved in their relationship. But he didn't want to come for marriage counseling until he checked me out. After I spent time listening to him and his perspective of his life and his marriage, he agreed to return for another session with his wife. I smiled and thought, *I passed.* Then, after he rose to leave, he plopped back in the chair, looked at me earnestly and said, "I guess the answer is I'll just have to fall more in love with myself."

I thought, *Is that true? Is the cause of Jonathan's depression and marital problems rooted in his lack of self-love?* For many years that's what we have been taught.

I could relate to what Jonathan said. Several years ago I was feeling miserable after the Lord had convicted me of my impatience with a particular person. In addition, I was brooding over some other mistakes I had made. Looking for some emotional support, I wandered into a colleague's office and unburdened myself. She said, "Leslie, stop being so hard on yourself. You can't love others well until you love yourself more. Sounds to me like you have a self-esteem problem." I nodded in agreement. But was that my real problem?

For a long time we have heard that high self-esteem and loving ourselves is essential to our well-being and happiness. One author of a best-selling book on self-esteem wrote, "I cannot think of a single psychological problem—from anxiety and depression, to fear of intimacy or of success, to spouse battery or child molestation—that is not traceable to the problem of poor self-esteem."[1] When I was in graduate school in the seventies, a popular slogan went something like this: "You can't love anyone else until you learn to love yourself first." Many Christians bought into this mind-set and taught that Jesus said we must learn to love ourselves *first* before we can love others *well.* (See Christ's command to love God and love others in Matthew 22:37-39.)

It is time we reexamine this idea more closely. Is more self-love or higher self-esteem the pathway to deeper intimacy with God, good relationships with others, inner satisfaction, and personal well-being? Or is there a different road altogether?

What Is Self-Image, Self-Esteem, and Self-Love?

Before going on, I think it is important to define the terms *self-image, self-esteem,* and *self-love.* For a long time, when people came to me for counseling and told me that they suffered from low self-esteem or a poor self-image or didn't love themselves, I wasn't quite sure what they had in mind. Did it mean she didn't like herself? Or maybe he didn't feel important or lacked self-confidence. Often people expressed that they felt worthless or inferior to others.

All of the above might indicate problems with the self. Yet, for the purpose of clarity, let's distinguish these terms from one another. This will help us better understand the essential quality of each component and see how our self-concept affects our lives and our relationships with others and with God.

Self-Image

Simply stated, our self-image is our mental picture of ourselves. When you think of yourself, what consistently comes to mind? Do you usually see someone who is competent, attractive, interesting, important, gifted, skilled, loved, and valued? Or perhaps more often you view yourself as incapable, unworthy of love, stupid, incompetent, ugly, or inferior to others. Our internal picture of ourselves begins to be shaped early in childhood by significant people in our lives who reflect back to us how they see us. In addition, our self-image is formed by the evaluations we make of ourselves. Over time, these internal mental pictures are solidified into our self-image. Ideally, these reflections and evaluations provide a relatively truthful representation of who we are, but sadly, they often don't.

Many times these distorted reflections and false evaluations lead us to make some inaccurate or untruthful conclusions about who we are. For example, Sally was the ninth child of an exhausted mother and father who did not believe in birth control. Her mother often passed her off to her older siblings to feed and care for her. Sally's parents rarely spoke to her, and she grew up with the impression that she was unloved and unimportant—that she didn't matter much. Sally's internal picture about who she was affected her feelings about herself and the decisions she made throughout adolescence. She gravitated toward needy people, because she believed that unless she could do something for them, they would not want to be her friend. Sally married a man who used her to take care of his needs but didn't give much consideration or thought to Sally's needs. Of course, why would he? She was unlovable and unimportant. Sally's negative self-image was based on perceptions of herself that she gained as a child that were powerful but untrue. In order to heal and grow so she could understand who she really was, Sally would need to see herself as God saw her.

On the other hand, Greg was an only child, a much-wanted baby after a ten-year battle with infertility. His parents doted on his every whim and constantly told him that he was wonderful, special, and capable of anything that he set his mind to. Greg grew up believing that he was loved and valued. He also believed that others should always want to please him, affirm him, and do whatever he wanted. Greg saw himself as a cut above others. Later on, when Greg's wife tried to express her needs or ideas, Greg felt slighted. After all, his needs should come first; he was the most important. Greg's inflated self-image was just as injurious to his well-being and future relationships as Sally's. For Greg to mature, he, too, would need to reevaluate how he saw himself—from God's perspective.

Both Greg and Sally had inaccurate or false pictures of themselves. Sally thought herself inferior to others; Greg believed himself superior. Sally saw herself as unlovable; Greg felt entitled to everyone's love and attention. Greg's and Sally's distorted self-images led to problems in their relationships with others and with God. Sally was afraid God wasn't interested in her; Greg used God as a servant to meet his needs and wishes. Neither was happy or content.

I have described two extremes, but most of us fall somewhere between the Gregs and Sallys of this world. No one grows up with a totally accurate self-image. But no matter how distorted or how inaccurate your picture of yourself is, I have good news for you: God's Word provides clear and truthful information about who we are so that we can begin to make corrections. I will explore this more fully in later chapters. For now, understand that this mental shift in our self-image is absolutely essential to our well-being, because how we think about ourselves or see ourselves has much to do with the related concept of self-esteem.

What Is Self-Esteem?

Whereas self-image may be described as the way we *think* about ourselves, self-esteem is the way we *feel* about ourselves. Our thoughts influence our feelings. Therefore it stands to reason that if we are thinking negatively about who we are, we will also feel negatively about ourselves. Sally didn't only think of herself as unlovable or unimportant; she also *felt* unlovable and unimportant. Sally never offered her opinion to others, because she didn't feel she had a perspective worth listening to. She always felt shy and insecure around other people because she saw herself as inferior.

On the other hand, Greg felt good about himself and had a lot of self-confidence. He had high self-esteem but low regard for others. He lacked compassion, was often demanding and self-centered, and became angry when others didn't see things his way or do what he wanted. Greg thought highly of himself and felt positively about himself—

qualities that most of us would value and think necessary to our personal happiness and well-being. Yet Greg was not satisfied. People never met his needs as adequately as he thought they should.

Sometimes we work hard to change our mental picture of ourselves but continue to feel poorly about our value and our worth. We can admit our strengths, see our assets, appreciate our talents or skills, but still feel insignificant or unimportant. We acknowledge that God made us and that God loves us, but that old feeling of being worthless or unlovable still gnaws at us from inside. This usually occurs when we have a head-heart split. In other words, we know (or acknowledge) the truth about who God says we are, but deep down, we don't really believe it or feel it.

I have two children, Ryan and Amanda. I love them both dearly. Ryan is my biological child; Amanda we adopted as an infant from Korea. When we adopted her, she became a Vernick. We gave her a new name, and her status was changed. She was no longer an alien from another country. As an American citizen, she was afforded the full rights and privileges of that identity. She was no longer an orphan; she had become our daughter. She was no longer penniless but had resources at her disposal for all of her needs and many of her wants. She was no longer alone; she was part of a family. She was no longer unloved or unwanted, but was dearly loved and deeply wanted.

Amanda experiences her identity in line with these realities. When she was little, she felt free to snuggle in my bed if she was frightened by a nightmare. Now that she's older, she doesn't think twice about running into my bathroom to use my hair gel or cosmetics or to borrow some jewelry. She knows she is adopted but fully trusts she is our daughter and is emotionally bonded to that truth.

But what if Amanda knew intellectually she was adopted but

emotionally felt unsure of our commitment to her? Because of her lack of trust, she might choose to sleep on the floor instead of in her nice big bed. She could be reluctant to eat our food or use our things. She might fear that if she displeased us we would send her back to Korea. What if Amanda thought we loved Ryan more than we loved her? If Amanda wasn't emotionally secure in her identity as our daughter or didn't trust that our covenant of adoption with her was meaningful, then her internal feelings would not align with the legal information she has about her adoption. She would experience her life (or feel) as if she were still an orphan, even though factually she is a Vernick.

Many of us fail to experience a change in our feelings about ourselves when we come to Christ for salvation, because we don't really believe God when he tells us we are his adopted children and that we are deeply loved and valued. We have head knowledge of those truths but lack heart trust. Those of us who suffer from this kind of head-heart split experience a great deal of emotional pain. We long to feel differently, to experience our adoption as children of God. We yearn to feel special, loved, and valued. If only we could really believe that God loves us, then maybe we could feel happy.

The writer of Hebrews spoke of this head-heart split when he told the Hebrew believers that they didn't experience God's peace and rest because they didn't really believe his promises (Hebrews 4:2). God knows our pain and turmoil, and he offers to heal us. However, our approach to healing our identity issues is crucial. We can't change these damaging feelings about ourselves by working on feeling better about ourselves. We only change our feelings when we deepen our trust and belief in God, and when our view of ourselves becomes aligned with God's view of us. Then the truth of our identity is not mere information but a heartfelt reality.

Self-Love

The last concept is closely related to the other two and might be defined simply as the way we treat ourselves. When Jesus tells us to "love your neighbor as yourself" (Luke 10:27), he is teaching us to care for our neighbor in the same good way that we would care for ourselves. John Piper wrote, "The self-love Jesus speaks of has nothing to do with the common notion of self-esteem. It does not mean having a good self-image or feeling especially happy with oneself. It means simply desiring and seeking one's own good."[2]

Scripture tells us, "No one ever hated his own body, but he feeds and cares for it" (Ephesians 5:29). In our humanity, we naturally love ourselves. The Lord doesn't say this is sinful, but it is automatic and necessary so that we will be responsible for our well-being. For example, when I cut my finger with a sharp knife, everything within me springs into action. My mind races to figure out what to do, my other hand applies pressure to my bleeding finger, my eyes begin to tear, and my voice cries out for help, all of which work together to comfort and care for my injured finger. Whenever I am criticized or corrected, my first impulse is to withdraw, to shut down and protect myself. Or sometimes out of love for myself I do the opposite: I go on the offensive and verbally retaliate in order to defend my wounded ego.

We all behave in ways that we believe will help us feel better when we're hurt or upset. Some of us take a nap or exercise. Others work on constructive problem solving or self-improvements. Even people who don't feel good about themselves or suffer from low self-esteem or poor self-images love themselves. Their behavior may look more like self-hatred than self-love because it appears to be destructive (like compulsive overeating, substance abuse, or promiscuity). However, people often engage in these destructive behaviors because they honestly believe these things will help them feel better, even if only temporarily.

The Bible tells a story of a young man who wanted to know what he needed to do to receive eternal life (Matthew 19:16-22). Jesus told him that he needed to keep the commandments. Then he got specific, ending with "and 'love your neighbor as yourself.'" The rich young man replied, "All these I have kept. What do I still lack?" But Jesus knew this young man's heart. The young man didn't have any problem loving himself, but he lacked love for God and his neighbor. To expose him, Jesus told the young man to "go, sell your possessions and give to the poor, and you will have treasure in heaven. Then come, follow me." The young man turned away. He loved himself and his money more than he loved God or his neighbor.

We often think of this parable as a story about money, but it is really a story about love—self-love gone awry. Thomas à Kempis wisely said, "We deceive our own selves through the inordinate love we have for the flesh."[3]

"What do I need to do to be happy?" could easily have been the question the rich young ruler asked Jesus that day. I believe Christ's answer would have been the same: *Let go of what you think makes you happy, and follow me.*

Because all people intrinsically love themselves, we all look for ways to satisfy ourselves and make ourselves happy. This is life's motivational drive. Blaise Pascal, a mathematician and philosopher said:

All look for happiness without exception. Although they use different means, they all strive toward this objective. That is why some go to war and some do other things. So this is the motive for every deed of man, including those who hang themselves.[4]

The Problem with the Pursuit of Self

One of the results of our cultural emphasis on promoting greater self-love and self-esteem is that we now believe we must find ourselves, feel good about ourselves, and fulfill ourselves so that we can be more self-confident, have more self-worth, and become self-sufficient and self-reliant. Elementary schools have implemented programs to raise students' self-esteem, and we who are parents vigilantly try not to damage our children's self-worth. Counselors have caseloads full of people who describe themselves as having low self-esteem, and bookstores devote a significant amount of shelf space to books on self-improvement, self-esteem, self-confidence, and the like.

A look at this idea from a biblical point of view leads to a surprisingly different conclusion. The Bible never encourages us to pursue loving ourselves or to work on enhancing our self-esteem at all. In fact, God's Word often cautions us against thinking too highly of ourselves (Romans 12:3) or too much of ourselves (Philippians 2:2-3). One of the central themes woven throughout the Scriptures is that of losing ourselves and dying to ourselves, not of loving ourselves.

It is time to carefully examine whether our cultural emphasis on the self has resulted in greater personal happiness, better relationships with others, and a deeper intimacy with God. Secular research examining the effects of self-esteem improvement efforts has yielded some startling results. A 1986 California task force found a low correlation between low self-esteem and poor behavior. In fact, the opposite was discovered. For example, they reported that many child abusers did not have low self-esteem. Nor did people on welfare.[5] Another study suggests that some of the most dangerous people are those who have a strong desire to regard themselves as superior beings and have an inflated self-image.[6]

These secular studies confirmed some of what I observed in my counseling practice. More often than not, people who experience discouragement, marital problems, and difficulties with anger management usually aren't suffering from a low opinion of themselves. Often it is just the opposite! They experience problems in living because they have strong feelings of entitlement and feel upset because people don't give them what they believe they deserve. Oswald Chambers wrote, "Discouragement rises from following self-love, and from nothing else. We get discouraged because we do not get our way."[7]

Is it possible that we've been getting it backward? Perhaps our difficulties in life occur, not because we don't think highly *enough* of ourselves, but because we think *too highly* and *too much* of ourselves. Our problems in life usually don't stem from loving *ourselves* too little, but of *loving others and God* too little and ourselves too much. Psychologist Paul Vitz said, "For the Christian the self is the problem, not the potential paradise."[8]

Love God More, Self Less

The fundamental questions in the heart of every human being are "Who am I?" and "Why am I here?" The answers we settle on will depend upon which lens we look through: the world's lens or God's. The world teaches us that to live well, we must focus more and more attention on loving our self by affirming that "I am" and "I can."

The irony is that when we pursue the path of self-discovery, self-fulfillment, or self-love, Jesus says we will ultimately lose ourselves. Paul reminds us that in the last days: "People will be *lovers of themselves,* lovers of money, boastful, proud, abusive, disobedient to their parents, ungrateful, unholy, without love, unforgiving, slanderous, without self-control, brutal, not lovers of the good, treacherous, rash, conceited, *lovers of pleasure* rather than *lovers of God*—having a form of godliness but denying its power. Have nothing to do with them" (2 Timothy 3:2-5, emphasis added).

The way to finding our true self begins by looking to God. Then we will get a much clearer picture of who we are and why we exist. We will cover this more extensively in later chapters, along with what constitutes a healthy self-image and what exactly biblical self-esteem and self-love look like. Contrary to the world's advice, the Lord tells us that only he can give us a fulfilling life because he alone is the great I AM. The path he calls us to involves denying our self and loving him with all of our heart, mind, strength, and will (Mark 12:30). God wants us to understand who we are and to look at all of life from his perspective (Proverbs 3:5-6) so that we will discover the secret of lasting joy. He is the Creator and Author of life, and only he knows what will satisfy our deepest longings. We were created by him and for him. Our souls are hungry, craving something that will truly satisfy our longings, but our spiritual taste buds have been dulled. Seeking gratification, we stuff ourselves with junk food, looking for something—anything—to quench the hunger in our souls. But we never quite experience satisfying fullness.

In our ignorance and sometimes in our rebellion, we strike out on our own, thinking that we know best what will fulfill our deepest longings. C. S. Lewis wrote that we are "half-hearted creatures, fooling about with drink and sex and ambition when infinite joy is offered us, like an ignorant child who wants to go on making mud pies in a slum because he cannot imagine what is meant by the offer of a holiday at the sea. We are far too easily pleased."[9]

Only God understands the desires of our heart, and he doesn't want us to settle for less than his best. He says, "Taste and see that the LORD is good" (Psalm 34:8). "He fulfills the desires of those who fear him" (Psalm 145:19). Instead of self-confidence, we need greater God-confidence, for he alone knows what will make us truly happy, truly satisfied.

PERSONAL APPLICATION

God never instructs us to concentrate on loving ourselves as a means of emotional or spiritual growth. He tells us deeper maturity comes about through loving and obeying him (see Matthew 6:33; John 15:10-11). In what ways have you been too focused on yourself and not enough on God or others? Begin to ask yourself and God how you might change this.

The Happiness Paradox

He is no fool who gives what he cannot keep
to gain what he cannot lose.

JIM ELLIOT

Adam sat in my office with tears streaming down his cheeks.
"Leslie, I have a great job, three beautiful children, a big expensive home, a wife who loves me, and plenty of money. I own three cars—just for me! But I'm still not happy. What is wrong with me?"

Good question. No one is more concerned with our happiness and well-being than Jesus is. Perhaps we should begin examining Adam's query with a look at what constitutes God's idea of inner happiness. When the Bible speaks of happiness or joy, it is not simply referring to the temporary pleasure that comes from having a great time on vacation or enjoying a delicious meal. Joy is not even the inner satisfaction we feel when we do a good job or the pleasure we experience when we gather together as a family for a holiday celebration. Those are all wonderful feelings, but they are fleeting, meant only to be tastes of something that points us toward the greatest pleasure and joy of all—knowing the presence of God.

Neither is biblical joy a state of mind where we wear a permanent smile and never feel sad. Jesus is described as a man of sorrows, acquainted with grief (Isaiah 53). Genuine happiness, joy, and a sense of contentment come when you know that your life is full—not of yourself, or of things, or even of other people—but full of God no matter what your circumstances (Psalm 21:6). Charles Spurgeon said, "To know Him is 'life eternal,' and to advance in the knowledge of Him is to increase in happiness."[1]

Like Adam, many of us relentlessly pursue happiness, and in the process we gain many wonderful material or temporal blessings. But those things do not fill our soul or provide lasting or deep satisfaction. The psalmist reminds us that happiness is never found when we seek it. Rather, happiness comes as a by-product of pursuing an upright life (Psalm 97:11). Jesus confirms this when he teaches us, "Blessed [or happy] are those who hunger and thirst for righteousness, for they will be filled" (Matthew 5:6). All of us hunger and thirst after those things that we believe will satisfy the cravings of our soul. However, many of us feast at the table of cheap substitutes, hungering and thirsting after power or money or attention or even happiness itself instead of righteousness, thus missing the sense of well-being and satisfaction that God offers us.

Jesus shows his followers the pathway to a happy and satisfied heart. He tells us what makes life meaningful and rich. It is just so contrary to what the world says, so paradoxical to our own way of thinking, that even most of us who call ourselves Christians don't actually believe it.

Jesus warns us not to live for temporal pleasures. He knows we will be happiest when we love God and live our lives in harmony with our created purpose. He not only sees where we are now, but he also sees beyond that to our true selves—what he has made us for.

Christ tells us that this process of finding our true selves and

genuine happiness begins with an accurate appraisal of our true condition: admitting that we are poor in spirit.

BLESSED (HAPPY) ARE THE POOR IN SPIRIT

How can we be happy if we are poor in spirit? As do many of God's
promises, this one appears to contradict itself.

Being poor in spirit does not mean that we should be timid, self-
deprecating, weak, or lacking in courage. Neither is poor in spirit
something that some people naturally have and others don't. Those
who possess a more modest and sedate personality may appear poor in
spirit, while those who are more jubilantly tempered may not. However, being poor in spirit as Jesus describes has nothing to do with
inborn temperament or personality. Being poor in spirit means that
you recognize your actual condition before God. You acknowledge
that you are nothing without him and that you need him in order to
be forgiven and to experience real joy and satisfaction in life.

Let's look more closely at *why* Jesus tells us that the poor in spirit
are the happiest or most satisfied. When someone is desperately poor,
it's hard to pretend otherwise. He knows his situation and his neediness. Some individuals who struggle with financial poverty may try to
hide that reality through the use of credit cards so that others do not
know the depths of their situation. But the one who is poor knows it,
even if others don't. However, by the world's standards, being poor
usually does not result in being happy. Often it's the opposite: We
might feel ashamed, angry, or sad because of our poverty.

Use your imagination with me for a moment. What if the news
networks announced tomorrow that a wealthy benefactor donated billions of dollars to help people in poverty. Every poor head of household in this country would receive a free home and a college education

or job training. An individual retirement account for twenty thousand dollars would be established in each one's name, and in addition, they would be given a start-up income of fifty thousand dollars a year for five years until they got on their feet. How many individuals would suddenly be quite happy to confess the truth of their condition, that they indeed were poor? What made the difference between those who felt ashamed or angry about their poverty and those who cheerfully embraced it? In our imaginary scenario, it was the fact that their poverty enabled them to receive an extravagant gift that they did not deserve or could not earn by themselves. The only requirement was that they had to acknowledge their poverty.

Like the wealthy benefactor, Jesus offers us something that will make us exceedingly happy—the kingdom of heaven. When Jesus describes the kingdom of heaven, he often uses a word picture. For example, he says, "The kingdom of heaven is like treasure hidden in a field. When a man found it, he hid it again, and then in his joy went and sold all he had and bought that field. Again, the kingdom of heaven is like a merchant looking for fine pearls. When he found one of great value, he went away and sold everything he had and bought it" (Matthew 13:44-46). Jesus tells us that it is not our poverty itself that makes us happy, but that confessing our poverty enables us to receive the treasures of God, whereby we will find our soul's true satisfaction.

Jesus tells us this wonderful, glorious gift is only available to those who will first admit that they need it and have no means to obtain it by themselves. We are all poor in spirit, whether or not we recognize or admit our poverty.

The world believes the opposite. *Think good thoughts about your-self. Say your affirmations, take care of yourself, and please and fulfill yourself first. Then you will find your true self and be happy.* In his book *The Psychology of Self-Esteem*, psychologist Nathaniel Branden says:

If a patient must be taught that the frustrations, the despair, the wreckage of his life are ultimately traceable to his deficiency of self-esteem and to the policies that led to that deficiency, it is equally imperative that he be taught the solution: that supreme expression of selfishness and self-assertiveness which consists of holding his self-esteem as his highest value and most exalted concern—and of knowing that each struggling step upward, taken in the name of that value, carries him further from the bondage to his past suffering and closer to the sunlit reality of the human potential.[2]

Christ clearly draws a line in the sand between the world's perspective and God's. We must decide which viewpoint we will embrace, which we will trust to bring us happiness. Jesus clearly tells us what we must do to reach our fullest potential: We must empty ourselves and believe that we cannot fill ourselves with anything of eternal value apart from God. Martin Lloyd-Jones says being poor in spirit "means a complete absence of pride, a complete absence of self-assurance and of self-reliance. It means a consciousness that we are nothing in the presence of God."[3] In order to be rich in Christ, we must first recognize the abject poverty in ourselves. We cannot possibly be filled up with the Spirit of God if we are already filled up with ourselves, whether positively or negatively.

To Discover Our True Selves, We Must First Deny Ourselves

Jesus also teaches, "If anyone would come after me, he must deny himself and take up his cross daily and follow me. For whoever wants to save his life will lose it, but whoever loses his life for me will save it.

What good is it for a man to gain the whole world, and yet lose or forfeit his very self?" (Luke 9:23-25). This is another one of those paradoxes that does not make sense to our human understanding. It collides with what the world sanctions. But what does Jesus mean when he tells us to die to ourselves or to deny ourselves? Years ago, I would give up eating ice cream for a while or tell myself I couldn't buy a certain outfit I wanted. I thought that I was denying myself.

In contrast to my trivial self-denials, others mistakenly think that dying to self means they should have no individual preferences, no personality differences, or anything that makes them unique as human beings. Somehow they believe that all mature Christians are to resemble one another and look like one big, happy smiley face. But God created us all unique, as individual portraits of his handiwork. Maturity shouldn't mean being absorbed into one big undifferentiated mass; rather, it should greatly enhance both us and the body of Christ, which was created to comprise diverse members.

To deny one's self in the Greek language means to refuse one's self or to give up one's self. The *NIV Study Bible* explains denying self this way: It means a person will "cease to make self the object of his life and actions."[4] In other words, we must die to our prideful, natural, self-centered, and selfish or self-conscious selves in order to live in the Spirit. The irony is that as we willingly do this, Jesus tells us that we will end up finding our true selves.

For Christ's followers, denying and dying to ourselves is not a request; it is a command. Why does Jesus give us such a difficult command? He doesn't leave us to wonder; in this same passage he tells us why. Jesus says, in essence, *I tell you this because I really want you to find your life, and you will never find your life in your self. Life is found only in me.* Jesus isn't saying we should become a nonperson as a follower of his. He is saying, *I want you to find out who you really are—the person I have created you to be. In order to do that, however, you must first deny the self you have created, the one that is your independent, prideful self. You must put that part of yourself on the cross daily and follow me.*

The apostle Paul reinforces Christ's words with his teachings. He tells us that because Christ died for us, we who live should no longer live for ourselves, but for him who died for us (2 Corinthians 5:15). In Colossians, Paul says something similar when he encourages believers to set their hearts and minds on things above rather than on earthly things. Why? Because "you died" Paul says, "and your life is now hidden with Christ in God." Paul continues, "Put to death, therefore, whatever belongs to your earthly nature" (Colossians 3:3,5). And in Paul's classic proclamation, he says, "I have been crucified with Christ and I no longer live, but Christ lives in me. The life I live in the body, I live by faith in the Son of God, who loved me and gave himself for me" (Galatians 2:20).

What Self Must We Die To?

We Must Die to Self-Sufficiency and Self-Reliance

A self-sufficient person is typically seen as a competent and emotionally healthy individual. After all, no one likes to be needy. And, in truth, a part of human maturity is learning what we can do so that we don't become overly dependent on others for what we should be doing ourselves. A child around the age of two begins to feel this sense of individuation when he tests the little word *no* and begins to try things on his own. One of my son's favorite phrases at that age was "I can do it myself." What that meant was, whether he got his shirt on backward or food smeared from his eyebrows to his chin, Ryan was determined to meet his own needs and not accept any help from Mom or Dad.

This process of growth is crucial. In order to mature, Ryan needed to find out what he was and was not capable of doing for himself. Part of my role as his mom was to allow him the space to discover his abilities and to help him recognize his limitations. However, in his classic book *A Serious Call to a Devout and Holy Life*, William Law cautions parents: "The first temper that we try to awaken in children is pride; as dangerous a passion as that of lust. We stir them up to vain thoughts of themselves, and do everything we can to puff up their minds with a sense of their own abilities."[5] Law's warnings came 250 years before our culture's emphasis on building up a child's self-esteem.

As we teach our children about their strengths, it is equally important for us also to teach them the truth. All of their talents and abilities are gifts from God, to be used for the benefit of others, not to feed their own egos. We must help them grasp that they will never be able to master their sin nature by themselves, nor will they ever be good enough to earn a relationship with God. They cannot remove the guilt for their sins, nor can they totally control their own future or grasp the big picture of life by themselves. Proverbs tells us, "Do you see a man wise in his own eyes? There is more hope for a fool than for him" (Proverbs 26:12).

Back in the garden, what appealed to Eve was this notion of self-sufficiency. *Gee, if I become like God, then I won't need God.* Ever since the Fall, our nature has been bent toward independence from God and the idea that we can live perfectly fine without him.

The Bible tells us, "Moses was educated in all the wisdom of the

Egyptians and was powerful in speech and in action. When Moses was forty years old, he decided to visit his fellow Israelites. He saw one of them being mistreated by an Egyptian, so he went to his defense and avenged him by killing the Egyptian. Moses thought that his own people would realize that God was using him to rescue them, but they did not" (Acts 7:22-25). Moses sensed God's calling in his life, yet he lacked one important quality—humility. Moses used his own strength when he defended the Israelite and killed the Egyptian. He was full of himself—full of power, self-confidence, and his own abilities. God couldn't use Moses that way. It took the next forty years of desert life for God to teach Moses humility. Only then was he ready to be who God had created him to be—the deliverer for Israel (see Exodus 2–3). Moses went from arrogant self-confidence to having no confidence in himself at all. It was here that he learned to depend upon God for his every word. Only when Moses was at the end of himself was God ready to give Moses a holy boldness to confront Pharaoh and lead the Israelites out of bondage. The apostle Paul learned the same thing when he realized, "When I am weak, then I am strong" (2 Corinthians 12:10).

When we believe that we are self-sufficient, our heart automatically and unconsciously grows proud, and we forget God. He warned Israel, "When you have eaten and are satisfied, praise the LORD your God for the good land he has given you. Be careful that you do not forget the LORD your God.... Otherwise, when you eat and are satisfied, when you build fine houses and settle down, and when your herds and flocks grow large and your silver and gold increase and all you have is multiplied, then your heart will become proud and you will forget the LORD your God, who brought you out of Egypt, out of the land of slavery" (Deuteronomy 8:10-14).

We Must Die to Our Self-Righteousness

Self-righteousness usually manifests itself in one of two ways. The first is a tendency to think that our way of seeing things is the only way to see them. As a result, we become proud of our convictions or our point of view, and we judge others who do not agree with us as wrong or sinful.

Maggie's family attended a conservative church that believed women should wear dresses only, especially to church services. They posted a sign on the door informing visitors of their convictions. Maggie's non-Christian grandmother lived far away and came for a visit. She always wore pants, no dresses ever. Maggie's parents went to the pastor of the church and told him of their desire to bring Grandma to church, but they knew she wouldn't wear a dress and feared she would leave if she saw the sign on the door. They asked their pastor if he would be willing to remove the sign for the Sunday that Grandma was in town. "Absolutely not!" their pastor said. "We will not compromise our convictions for anyone." How sad. This pastor seemed more concerned about his convictions than Grandma's relationship with Christ.

Oswald Chambers warned, "Perhaps the most subtle false standard of spirituality arises from a selfish adherence to one's own convictions."[6] The Pharisees, too, were convinced of the rightness of their point of view. Tragically, it blinded them to their own need for Jesus and the forgiveness he offered. The Bible says that there are "those who are pure in their own eyes and yet are not cleansed of their filth; those whose eyes are ever so haughty, whose glances are so disdainful" (Proverbs 30:12-13). Jesus wanted the world to know us by our love, not by our stringent adherence to personal convictions. Self-righteousness mars the beauty of Christ in us.

The second form of self-righteousness we must die to is our tendency to compare ourselves to others and believe that we're better than they are. Jesus told a story about the prayers of two men, a Pharisee and a sinner (Luke 18:9-14). The Pharisee, confident of his own righteousness, looked down at others, thanking God that he was not like them. He was proud of his achievements and good works in the synagogue. The sinner simply looked up at God, pleading for mercy. Jesus said, "I tell you that this man, rather than the other, went home justified before God. For everyone who exalts himself will be humbled, and he who humbles himself will be exalted" (verse 14).

At times we, too, act like Pharisees. We see someone struggle with a more public sin, and we cluck our tongue, shake our finger, or turn up our nose. We feel holier, more righteous. We say to ourselves, *I would never do such a thing.* Others may look at people in their congregation and think, *I'm glad I don't drink or smoke or watch the television programs or listen to the kind of music that so-and-so does. I'm more holy, more righteous.* Be careful. Scripture warns us, "For in his own eyes he flatters himself too much to detect or hate his sin" (Psalm 36:2). We may each manifest our sins in different ways, but God says we are all sinners. Seeing ourselves truthfully helps us realize that we are no better or more important than anyone else.

We Must Die to Our Self-Consciousness and Morbid Introspection

It is quite possible to be just as self-absorbed with our faults and failures as with our strengths and accomplishments. (We will learn more about this problem of the self in chapter 4.) While some introspection is necessary for healthy self-examination, many of us endlessly scrutinize ourselves, examining every thought, every word, and every action for flaws, sins, weaknesses, or mistakes.

Kaitlyn sat wringing her hands and looking as though she had the cares of the world on her shoulders. When I inquired about the problem, she confessed, "I failed to claim something on my income taxes, and I'm afraid that God is displeased. I feel awful. I'd been worrying about this for over six months when I finally made an appointment to see you."

"What was it that you didn't claim, Kaitlyn?" I asked, imagining it to be a large lottery win or some other questionable source of income.

"Last year I walked for the Leukemia Foundation. I won some prizes for collecting donations. My accountant told me not to bother putting them on my tax return, but now I'm not so sure. I listened to him and didn't claim them as income, and now I'm upset with myself."

Curious, I asked her what she'd won. Kaitlyn replied, "A T-shirt, a poster, and a water bottle."

As I got to know Kaitlyn more, I found that she habitually fretted over her sins, flaws, and imperfections, both real and imagined. When we, like Kaitlyn, are morbidly introspective or self-conscious, we turn in on our self, analyzing and examining, always trying to explain, understand, or make sense of our lives. We become our own Holy Spirit, gazing inward, looking for flaws, and usually finding them.

Seventeenth-century mystic François Fénelon wisely warned us about this proclivity. He said, "Merely to see how wretched we are and to fall into despair over what we see is not being humble. On the contrary, to do that is to have a fit of pride that cannot consent to being brought low."[7] He also said, "Discouragement is not the fruit of humility, but of pride."[8] Gary Thomas suggests that when we are constantly anxious about or disappointed with ourselves, perhaps we have made an "idol out of our own piety."[9] To grow into the person God wants us to be, we need to die to our habit of constantly gazing at ourselves, being morbidly occupied, worried, and anxious about our performance or lack of perfection. Instead, we need to learn to take our eyes off ourselves and fix them on the perfection, beauty, and grace of God.

We Must Die to Our Self-Centeredness and Self-Indulgence

We've already talked about humankind's natural self-centeredness, but it is imperative that we move beyond an intellectual understanding of these things. We must now learn how to die to our desire for preeminence and our tendency to put ourselves at the center of everything. The Scriptures tell the story of a man who was greatly gifted with supernatural strength but was self-centered and lived for his own pleasure. (See Judges 13–16 for the story of Samson.) Samson's self-indulgence cost him. After he told Delilah the source of his supernatural strength, she betrayed him and had his head shaved as he slept. When he woke up, Samson thought he could shake free of his Philistines enemies like before. Not this time. Samson did not know that his source of strength (God) had left him. How tragic, not only that his strength left, but that Samson didn't even know that the source of that strength had left him. The Philistines gouged out his eyes, bound him with shackles, and humiliated him by giving him woman's work to do—grinding grain.

God has gifted each of us. He has created us with a purpose in mind so we might know him and so our lives might give him glory. Sadly, many of us live self-indulgently like Samson and use our abilities for self-centered purposes, forgetting that God is the source of our strength. Samson may have seemed happy, but like many of us, he never was satisfied. When we live to please our flesh, it becomes more demanding. Instead of leading us to contentment, it leaves us hungering for more. Dying to self-centeredness and self-indulgence is the only path that frees us from the bondage of our passions and appetites, enabling us to become our true self and find joy humbly serving others.

Death Leads to New Life

In his book *Into the Depths of God,* Calvin Miller wrote, "Self had to be denied, said Jesus. 'Crucified,' said Paul. Why? Because the self served only self. The ego thrives best in soil so shallow it can give no root to the purposes of God."[10] Again, we are only free to grow into our true selves when we die to our old way of being and yield ourselves to God's restorative work in our lives.

God often illustrates spiritual truths through his creation. Imagine a tiny acorn telling God, "Oh please, don't let that squirrel bury me in the ground. I don't want to die." God knows that an acorn must let go of its identity as an acorn in order to grow into the mighty tree that he designed it to become. Or how about a furry caterpillar arguing with God that it doesn't want to spin a cocoon and go to sleep? If it doesn't submit to God's plan, it will never be transformed into a beautiful butterfly. Unlike humankind, nature willingly surrenders itself to God's best.

We find it difficult to trust God in this process. We resist him and somehow foolishly believe that we're better off when we cling to our own way. But pride and sin degrade our true selves. It is only when we humble ourselves and die to our sinful pride that Jesus can begin the restoration process. Andrew Murray said, "Our pride came from Adam—our humility must come from Christ. Pride is ours and rules in us with such terrible power because it is our self, our essential nature. Humility must be ours in the same way; it must be our very self, our essential nature."[11] Oswald Chambers said, "Sanctification means being made one with Jesus so that the disposition that ruled Him will rule us. Are we prepared for what that will cost? It will cost everything that is not of God in us."[12] What do we gain in exchange?

The lovely nature of God—living within us (Ephesians 4:24; 2 Peter 1:4).

GAINING BY LOSING

I've always been fascinated with the true story of Helen Keller and Annie Sullivan as depicted in the movie *The Miracle Worker.* Helen Keller was born in 1880, and an illness during infancy left her blind, deaf, and unable to speak. Helen's parents were compassionate but clueless on how to reach her.

Helen appeared oblivious to her condition. Because she could neither see nor hear, she didn't comprehend language or what life was about. Helen's greatest pleasures were being rocked by her mother and having the freedom to grab fistfuls of food from family members' plates and mash it into her mouth whenever she pleased. But Helen knew nothing of feeding on the things that would nourish her mind or her soul. She was figuratively dead to those things. Helen's parents hired Annie Sullivan as a live-in teacher in the hope that somehow she could find a way to reach Helen and teach her words.

Annie's first task was to teach Helen some basic manners. Helen resisted, and out of pity, her family interfered with her lessons. Annie's methods may have looked harsh and heartless, but she needed to capture Helen's undivided attention so that she could be taught. If only Helen could learn words, an entire world would open up to her, a world that was beautiful and stimulating. Annie knew that sign language would provide Helen the opportunity to grow, to develop, and become all she was capable of being.

Helen fought Annie's instructions and rebelled against her teacher's love. Even so, Annie persisted, often repeating the same lesson again and again. In one particularly moving scene, Annie furiously pumps water into Helen's hand, forming the word W-A-T-E-R in her other hand. Repeatedly the teacher presses this precious word into Helen's palm. Then a spark ignites—a glimmer of understanding crosses Helen's face, and she tentatively presses the letters W-A-T-E-R back into Annie's palm. Annie excitedly nods and cups Helen's hands to her face. "Yes," she cries. Helen's appetite for words is born, and we see her hungrily seeking more and more words while Annie carefully presses each letter that makes the word into her open hand, nodding and laughing and crying, "Yes, yes, yes!"

Language was something Helen never could have imagined as a blind, deaf, and mute child. But because of Annie Sullivan's faithfulness and love, Helen Keller not only learned to read, write, and speak, but she went on to graduate cum laude from Radcliffe College in 1904. Helen Keller became an author, lectured worldwide, and received many honors and distinctions. She said, "I thank God for my handicaps, for through them, I have found myself, my work, and my God."[13]

Once she learned what Annie wanted to teach her, Helen Keller found joy, happiness, and purpose in life. Prior to Annie's involvement in her life, Helen Keller was dead to her true self.

God knows the end for which we were made. He knows how to

get us there if only we will yield ourselves to him and what he wants to teach us. Oswald Chambers tells us that "joy means the perfect fulfillment of that for which I was created and regenerated."[14]

Spiritually, I am like Helen Keller. I am blind, deaf, and mute. I don't understand or know how to speak God's language and am oblivious to what I am missing. But God reminds me that he has created me for more than I can think or even imagine. I am designed to reflect his glory, not my own. He shows me that his ways are better, but I will never see or know or experience them unless—until—I begin to get a glimpse of more *real* life than what I presently experience. Then, like Helen, I must yield myself fully to Jesus so that he can teach me what I need to learn and help me live it.

PERSONAL APPLICATION

What has God been telling you that you need to die to so he can become more? Is it your self-confidence or self-sufficiency? Maybe it is your tendency toward self-righteousness or your struggle with morbid introspection. Are you self-indulgent? It is difficult to trust God and let go of our own way of doing things, yet if we want to grow, we must yield our way to God's best. Begin right now. Write a prayer of surrender to God, giving him the opportunity to bring forth his image in you. For example:

> *Dear Lord, I see your way is best. I see what you*
> *are teaching me, but actually dying to myself is*
> *much harder than just thinking about it. Move*

these lessons from my head to my heart. Show me the areas in my life where I am too full of myself, where my pride rules me instead of your love. May the deepest desire of my heart be to know you and to love you and to please you in all I do. Amen.

Humility: What Is It, and Why Do We Avoid It?

So let us realize our limitations.
We are something
and we are not everything.

BLAISE PASCAL

Leading morning worship, the emcee greeted us with a big smile. "Laaadieees," she crowed, "repeat after me. God made me, and that makes *me* special. Goooooood! Let's say it again, this time louder—like you really mean it!"

Although I have no doubt that this worship leader meant well, the emphasis of her statement made me a little queasy. I fear we have twisted the familiar passage in Psalm 139 to say, *I will praise ME (instead of Thee), for I am fearfully and wonderfully made.* John Piper observes that in today's climate, "The ultimate sin is no longer the failure to honor and thank God but the failure to esteem oneself."[1] When we become the center of our own worship, we reduce God to the role of a useful servant in our quest to reach our personal goals.[2]

Somewhere in our search for a better self-image or improved self-esteem, we got lost. Much like the Greek nymph Narcissus, we have been peering into a pond, hoping to find love, meaning, and fulfillment in our own reflection. Calvin Miller wrote, "The tiniest of gods are to be found in the mirrors of egotists. Yet this little 'mirror of the me' is where most of the world's masses worship. They may occasionally peer past the edges of the mirror to see that there is a worthier vastness beyond it. But most continue to adore the little image of themselves, always asking at every turn, 'What's in this for me?'"[3] Stuart Briscoe warns, "Modern man's love affair with himself has produced such incredible self-centeredness that we are now variously called the 'me-first generation' or the 'narcissistic society.'"[4] Even as believers, we have become absorbed and consumed with ourselves—our needs, our interests, our goals, our feelings, and our thoughts, often describing our quest as a journey toward emotional health.

So what's wrong with believing in ourselves or working to enhance our self-esteem? What's wrong with our notions of self-confidence and self-sufficiency? The problem is that they are lies, and when we believe these lies, we live as if we are the main character in our story. Larry Crabb, addressing why people today have so many problems, concludes, "It all comes down to self-centeredness, to a naturally self-focused, self-reliant soul that we're powerless to change. We place our interests above God's; we plot ways to use God for our agendas; and we refuse to recognize God's glory as the final value we can joyfully pursue."[5] Life then is not about glorifying, satisfying, or obeying the one true God, but about pleasing ourselves.

The truth is, God is not only the author of our story; he is the main character.

WORTHLESS WORMS AND WRETCHES

Many of us gag over the words of the old hymns that describe human-kind as worms, wretches, or worse. Instead of embracing humility as a worthy and desirable virtue, we fear it. We dread and despise it. We don't like to see ourselves as weak or worthless. We don't want to feel needy or desperate. We hate being told we are sinful or small. We want to be fine, good, healthy, and full of self-confidence. We long to be worthy, and we're insulted by the thought that we are incapable of being good in ourselves. The idea that humility has anything to do with joy or contentment is foreign to our minds. Yet, as we've already seen, unless we begin to see ourselves as destitute—poor in spirit—we lose our greatest spiritual blessing.

Humility has often been maligned and misunderstood. We have wrongly seen it as weakness and think that those who have it become doormats on which others wipe their feet. We disdain humility because we associate it with the searing pain of humiliation. In his classic book on humility, Andrew Murray properly defined humility as "simply acknowledging the truth of our position as human beings and yielding to God His place."[6] François Fénelon said, "Pure charity divests man of himself. It reclothes him with Jesus Christ. That is in what true humility consists, which makes us live no longer for our-selves, but lets Jesus Christ live in us."[7] In *The Glorious Pursuit,* Gary Thomas explains it this way: "Humility is not a positive or negative view of self as much as it is a *forgetfulness* of self."[8]

Simply put, humility is an accurate assessment of who we are and a heartfelt acknowledgment that anything good in us is a result of God's goodness in us. It is admitting that all we are that is admirable comes from God, and therefore he gets the praise and the glory.

Genuine humility is always accompanied by an inner attitude of deep submission to the lordship of Christ and a detachment from the desire for personal praise or recognition. The outward manifestation of this inward change is an absence of self-consciousness and an attitude of self-forgetfulness that enables a person to love others and serve them with the love of Christ without asking, "What's in it for me?" or, "How am I doing?"

Throughout the rest of the book I will seek to unpack this definition so that we can grasp more fully how central selflessness is to a joy-filled life and personal and relational happiness.

Authentic Humility Grows Out
of an Accurate Assessment of Who We Are

In high school Tom was a star. Since he was six foot two inches tall and the top basketball player for his team, everyone looked up to him and admired his talents and abilities. He had his pick of girlfriends, many friends, and was the senior class president.

But when Tom showed up at his ten-year high school reunion, he looked different to his peers. He wasn't so big anymore. He hadn't liked college, so he had dropped out. Tom had been so accustomed to being the center of attention that he couldn't seem to make the transition to being a regular person at college. He returned to his hometown so he could be the big shot once again. Now, ten years later, he sells insurance and lives on his memories of what once was.

Have you ever felt like a big fish and then realized that the reason you looked big was because you were in a small pond? It can be a humbling experience. Like Tom, many of us see ourselves in a context that distorts our picture. When faced with new information about who we really are, we may feel humiliated. Instead of allowing this experience to humble us, however, we retreat to protect our false image. God often provides these humbling opportunities so that we can see ourselves rightly in order to grow and become the person he intended us to become.

Eva Marie, a friend of mine, recalled a time when she and her husband, through no fault of their own, lost their business and had to file for bankruptcy. "It was so humiliating, Leslie," Eva Marie shared. "I had always dressed in the latest labels, and now I found myself sitting in the welfare office asking for food stamps. I was filled with shame and would go grocery shopping after midnight. Yet," Eva Marie continued, "over time, God taught me so much. For one thing, I began to see that I had been proud and self-sufficient. I never saw myself as a proud person before this happened, but God used this experience to teach me the truth about myself in so many ways. Through it I began to learn what real humility was."

In chapter 1 we discussed the danger of self-love and the probability that we have developed an inaccurate picture of ourselves. When the apostle Paul speaks of having sober judgment about ourselves in Romans 12:3, the word he uses in the Greek simply means to have a sound mind or to assess ourselves honestly. Every day we rely on external truth tellers like mirrors or scales to give us an accurate assessment of our physical condition. Am I gaining too much weight? Do I have dirt on my face? Is my hair combed in the back? These truth tellers help us make corrections so that we can look our best.

But where do we find an accurate mirror in which to see our internal selves correctly? Someone has said, "The truest thing about you is what God says about you." God's Word is our mirror that accurately reflects who we are, what we were made for, and how we are to live our lives so that we become the people God created us to be. Let's look then at God's Word to see how he describes us.

We Are Created in His Image
and for Relationship with Him

Genesis 1:27 says, "So God created man in his own image, in the image of God he created him; male and female he created them." God stamped human beings with the indelible likeness of himself. Like God, we think, we feel, and we have the capacity for moral judgment and reasoning. We love justice, order, and beauty. The psalmist says that we are fearfully and wonderfully made (Psalm 139:14), and God said that his creation was very, very good.

From the beginning, God created humankind to be in an intimate relationship with himself. He loved us and designed us to be dependent upon his wisdom to navigate life successfully. Henry Nouwen says, "Our preciousness, uniqueness and individuality are not given to us by those who meet us in clock-time—our brief chronological existence—but by the One who has chosen us with an everlasting love, a love that existed from all eternity and will last through all eternity."[9]

Human beings are special to God. He created us with dignity, value, and purpose (Psalm 8:5-8). God did not make us worthless worms or wretches. In fact, he says he made us just a little lower than the angels and crowned us with his glory and honor. John Bevere wrote, "The Hebrew word for 'crowned' is *atar*. It means 'to encircle or surround.' In essence, the man and woman were clothed with the glory of the Lord and didn't need natural clothing."[10]

We Have Made a Terrible Exchange

Romans 1:21-23 says, "For although they knew God, they neither glorified him as God nor gave thanks to him, but their thinking became futile and their foolish hearts were darkened. Although they claimed to be wise, they became fools and exchanged the glory of the immortal God for images made to look like mortal man and birds and animals and reptiles."

Today we no longer enjoy the unbroken intimate relationship with God that he intended. The Bible tells us that our sin separates us from him (Isaiah 59:2). To understand sin as God sees it, we must go back to the beginning. Adam and Eve had a great life. They loved God and each other. There was no conflict, no sin, no shame. They knew themselves, each other, and God. They busily tended the garden God gave them and cared for the animals. Adam and Eve were happy and living fully as God intended. So what went wrong? What ruined their idyllic state? It began with a lie—a little lie that grew to have enormous consequences. Satan began to question what God had said. "Eve," the serpent challenged, "did God really say, 'You must not eat from any tree in the garden'?" (see Genesis 3).

The serpent wove his lies in such a way that he made them sound reasonable, even truthful. "Eve, you won't die if you eat that forbidden fruit," Satan promised. "For God knows that when you eat it, you will become like him, and he doesn't want that. God is trying to gyp you out of something that is good for you."

Satan's strategy isn't any different today. "Humility? That isn't healthy," Satan whispers. "Lower yourself? What about you? People will walk all over you or take advantage. Humble yourself? You're self-esteem is low enough. You can't possibly love others until you love yourself first. Forget yourself? You won't be happy unless you find yourself. If you don't make yourself happy, no one else will." We have all struggled with these thoughts, and our culture certainly reinforces them. Satan's goal is to tweak a lie so cleverly that it sounds reasonable, truthful, even right. Eve sinned the instant she chose her own way instead of God's way. The process started when she believed the serpent's lie rather than what God said. Eve began to desire what the serpent promised instead of being satisfied with what God provided. *Yes,* Eve thought to herself, *if I eat this fruit I will be like God. I won't have to depend on God's goodness and God's glory anymore. I will have my own!*

Once that decision was made, Adam and Eve changed. They were no longer clothed with God's glory, and they found themselves naked and ashamed. Instead of turning to God, Adam and Eve hid and made coverings for themselves out of fig leaves.

Consequently, we human beings are all born with an inner disposition that seeks independence from God. By nature we instinctively exchange God's glory—the glory that he designed for us in creation—for a cheap substitute, our own glory. (The Bible calls it our pride, and we will cover that more extensively in chapter 7.) Jeremiah, the weeping prophet, laments, "But my people have exchanged their Glory for worthless idols" (Jeremiah 2:11). The apostle Paul tells us that "all have sinned and fall short of the glory of God" (Romans 3:23). Ever since Adam and Eve, human beings have been committed to finding glory in themselves apart from God.[11]

All That Is Good in Us Is from God

"Don't be deceived, my dear brothers. Every good and perfect gift is from above, coming down from the Father of the heavenly lights, who does not change like shifting shadows" (James 1:16-17). "For who makes you different from anyone else? What do you have that you did not receive? And if you did receive it, why do you boast as though you did not?" (1 Corinthians 4:7).

Perhaps one of the reasons humility feels so distasteful is that we have misread Paul's words where he says, "I know that nothing good lives in me," and left out the last part, "that is, in my sinful nature" (Romans 7:18). Some people have been taught that there is nothing good in them at all. As a result they feel worthless and purposeless. Or they exhibit a false humility that denies the good gifts God has given them.

The truth is, there *is* good *in* us; it is just not *from* us. The good in us is from God. In spite of our sin, God has not removed his likeness from us. His goodness is still abundantly evident as he blesses humankind with gifts of talents, abilities, intelligence, and creativity. We can easily see beauty and imagination expertly expressed when we stroll through an art museum. Goodness is demonstrated through kindness and compassion when volunteers lovingly and tenderly care for the homeless, the elderly, or AIDS and hospice patients. And we only have to turn on a cell phone to marvel at the intelligence that created a tiny wireless box for talking with someone thousands of miles away. However, we often take the credit for these abilities and crave the glory for ourselves, as if these talents originated within us.

Dan worked for a company that valued good ideas. Employees were encouraged to submit their proposals for ways to improve production, cut costs, or streamline paperwork. Each month one employee's suggestion would be selected and implemented, and that person would be recognized as employee of the month and rewarded with a gift certificate to a fancy restaurant. One day Dan found out that an idea submitted by his coworker John was selected. John walked around the office beaming with pride. However, when John's suggestion was announced, Dan recognized it as his own. John robbed Dan not only of his idea but also of the recognition due him.

When we take credit for our talents, gifts, and abilities, we rob God of the glory due him and often fail to use those gifts in the manner

God intended. That is, we use our gifts and talents for self-serving purposes rather than to serve one another. We fail to recognize that apart from God's goodness toward us, we would not survive. Bernard of Clairvaux warned, "It is dangerous to presume that any good in us is the result of our own efforts. We become arrogant. Not only do we fail to give God the credit due him, we actually despise him."[12]

The gifts God bestows are not from us, nor are they for us so that we can feel good about ourselves. They are to be used to benefit others and glorify him (1 Peter 4:10).

Our Hearts Are Prone to Self-Deception

Jeremiah 17:9-10 says, "The heart is deceitful above all things and beyond cure. Who can understand it? I the LORD search the heart and examine the mind."

Galatians 6:3 says, "If anyone thinks he is something when he is nothing, he deceives himself." And 1 John 1:8: "If we claim to be without sin, we deceive ourselves and the truth is not in us."

Not only are we vulnerable to being deceived by Satan, we are quite good at deceiving ourselves. One of the reasons believing in ourselves is so foolish is that we cannot possibly know ourselves truthfully apart from God. God is the one who made us; he is the one who intimately knows us and understands all of our ways.

When Jesus predicted that all the disciples would desert him, Peter bragged, "Even if all fall away on account of you, I never will" (Matthew 26:33). Little did Peter know that in a few short hours, his own heart would be full of doubt, full of fear. But Jesus knew. Peter's failure marked the end of his self-sufficiency and self-confidence. That was a good thing, so he could learn to be dependent on God's strength, not his own.

Self-deception creeps into our hearts in a variety of ways. When I see something I desire, I can easily convince myself that I *need* it, when in reality I don't. Instead of calling myself lazy when I avoid a task I don't want to do, I tell myself I'm tired. After arguing with my husband, I can rationalize that he's at fault and should apologize first. *No, Lord, I'm not being proud or arrogant; I'm merely trying to communicate my point!*

Another way we deceive ourselves is by avoiding truth. Kathy is in debt, but she has no idea how much. She doesn't want to know, because if she faced it, she might be convicted to do something about it. When the bills come, she stuffs them unopened in a drawer. That way she convinces herself that it's not as bad as it really is. When we cultivate the habit of deceiving ourselves long enough, we can do some bad things and call them good. Rapists convince themselves that their victims enjoy being raped, and child molesters often tell themselves that the child was the initiator and wanted sexual contact. The Bible does not speak well of those who call good evil and evil good, who call dark light and light dark (Isaiah 5:20). James Houston says, "Unquestionably it is an evil to be so full of faults, but it is a still greater evil to be full of them and yet unwilling to acknowledge them, since this results in the further evil of deliberate self-delusion."[13]

God tells us that we are not capable of understanding ourselves or life apart from knowing him (Proverbs 3:5-6). Oswald Chambers said, "We have to get rid of the idea that we understand ourselves, it is the last conceit to go. The only One Who understands us is God. The greatest curse in spiritual life is conceit."[14] We prefer to believe the lies that sound so much like truth, because they make us feel better about ourselves.

Why would we want to take on such a huge task as to run our own life? Pride. Because God loves us, he brings us to a place where we have the opportunity to see the truth about who we are. The truth is, we are sinful people who are deeply loved and valued by God. Some of us don't experience our belovedness. Others of us don't recognize our brokenness. We haven't come to accept that we are not God. We have failed to understand that we don't have what it takes, that we don't know all we need to know, that we aren't as good as we thought we were, that we are poor in spirit, that we need him.

When we come to that place, we can begin to discover our true selves and our deepest joy. But before we can discover how to walk the path of selflessness, we first must take a look at some of the impostors of genuine humility.

Personal Application

In what ways have you doubted God and been unwilling to trust his Word for your life? Do you really think you know better than he does what you need? Ask him to give you a more accurate picture of yourself and the faith to believe him, not just believe *in* him.

4

Humility's Impostors

My sin is to look on my faults and be discouraged,

or to look on my good and be puffed up.

PURITAN PRAYER

M y husband and I live hundreds of miles away from the Mid-west, where our parents and siblings are. We are only able to visit about once or twice a year. The hardest times of separation always come around the holidays, when families usually spend time together. Over the years we have sometimes compensated for our loneliness by having our own "extended family" holiday celebrations. We would invite other "strays," as we called ourselves, to our home to share in Thanksgiving dinner, Fourth of July picnics, and New Year's Day parties. One couple, John and Sharon, became regulars, as their extended family also lived far away. Each holiday we joyfully welcomed this couple and others to our home. But after a few years, I began to feel a little resentful because in all this time, Sharon and John had never returned the invitation.

"Maybe they don't really like us," I confided to my husband during one of my more negative moments. "What if they're using us because they have nothing better to do?"

I hope that you are not plagued with such ridiculous thoughts about any of your friends. My husband, Howard, tried to reassure me, but once I opened the door to these doubts, they continued to march in uninvited. My negative thinking began to affect my feelings for Sharon. I could no longer smile at her when I said "Hi" or look her in the eye when I passed her at church. My strategy was to avoid her, and since our church is large, I could do so successfully for a time. Finally, during another one of my complaining sessions, my husband said, "Well if it bothers you that much, why don't you ask her?"

"And what am I supposed to say to her?" I moaned. 'Why haven't you invited us to your house for dinner?' That sounds really mature!"

"It's up to you," Howard wisely counseled, "but as I see it, you can either talk to her about it or let it go. The way you're handling it right now isn't doing anyone any good."

I gulped. I knew he was right, but I wasn't about to talk to her. Yet something (or Someone) kept tugging at my heart. *Go talk to her. Ask her.* Finally I prayed. "Lord, I don't want to talk to Sharon about this; I'd rather forget it. Please help me to let it go. But"—I added as an afterthought—"if for any reason you want me to speak with her, make it VERY obvious." The next Sunday I exited Sunday school down the back stairway to avoid you know who. And guess who was coming up the back stairway? Instantly I knew God had arranged this moment and that I was to speak to her about my feelings. I took a deep breath as my knees started knocking and my legs turned to Jell-O.

"Sharon, do you have a minute?"

"Sure, what's up?" She had no clue what I was about to unload.

Tears welled up in my eyes, and I could barely choke out the words. "Wh-wh-why after all this time haven't you ever invited us to your home?" I blurted. "Is there a problem in our relationship?"

Sharon looked stunned. When she composed herself, she said,

"Leslie, I'm really sorry. I didn't mean to hurt you. We never have anyone over. I've always been shy, and it's hard for me to make interesting
conversation. I can never think of what to say to people when I have
them over. Besides, my house is small, and I don't have the decorating
knack that you have. I'm not a good cook, and I feel inadequate entertaining. It's not you—it's me!"

IT'S ALL ABOUT ME: THE PROBLEM
WITH EXCESSIVE SELF-CONSCIOUSNESS

We first heard these four little words, *it's all about me,* in chapter 1,
where we saw that we have an innate tendency to worship ourselves—to put ourselves at the center of our story. At first glance,
Sharon's comments may appear self-effacing, even humble. After all,
Sharon isn't worshiping herself, nor is she thinking more highly of
herself. Rather, she has a fairly low opinion of herself—some might
say Sharon suffers from a poor self-image or low self-esteem. Yet the
problem that plagued us both is that we were still thinking too much
of ourselves. My self-absorption was in keeping score; Sharon's was in
her fear of not being able to communicate and to be an adequate
hostess. These fears kept her eyes locked on herself, her weaknesses,
her inadequacies, and her flaws instead ministering to others, loving
them as Christ calls her to. The Bible has a name for this, but it's
not "low self-esteem," "meekness," or "humility." It's called *the fear
of man.*

The reason excessive timidity may be mistaken for humility is
because a shy person like Sharon does not vie for personal attention
or recognition and is not looking for status or glory—all aspects of
a humble heart. However, for those who are plagued by inordinate
self-consciousness, there is no freedom in these actions. Their hearts

are not ruled by love but by fear. Oswald Chambers says, "Such conscientiousness is selfishness, inverted from glowing pride into a creeping fear."[1]

The apostle Paul told young Timothy, "God did not give us a spirit of timidity, but a spirit of power, of love and of self-discipline" (2 Timothy 1:7). The Greek word used here for *timidity* is *deilia*, which means "fearfulness." "The word denotes cowardice and timidity and is never used in a good sense."[2] Proverbs 29:25 tells us that the "fear of man will prove to be a snare." Although on the outside we may appear to be more humble than the person who is self-confident or self-seeking, our self-love works in a much more insidious way. It maneuvers to shield us against the possibility of failure, rejection, and disapproval.

Let's explore the kinds of fears that keep us internally locked up, hindered from becoming the people God designed us to be.

Fear of Failure

As Sharon and I talked further, my heart went out to her. I knew her fears—the same sort gripped my heart. Mine weren't in the area of entertaining and socializing but in the realm of writing. A number of years ago I was severely criticized about something I wrote. The judgment was so painful I doubted that I would ever put my pen to paper again. I told myself that others could communicate more eloquently than I and that God could easily find someone else to say what he was asking me to write. The truth is, there are better writers than I, and God can find someone else to do it if I don't want to trust him with what he is asking me to communicate. However, my self-effacing statements didn't flow from a humble heart but out of my wounded pride and fear of further criticism.

At first glance, a person who defers to others, hangs in the shadows, doesn't reach out, and refuses ministry responsibilities may appear humble. When we look closer, however, we will see that he or she is just as preoccupied with self and has as much self-love as the person who is outwardly selfish and self-centered. Self-love in the outwardly selfish person manifests in prideful demands, in the "humble" person in a self-protective withdrawal. My friend Lois once told me, "Self-love is always self-love, whether it parades as pride and importance or masquerades as self-pity, worthlessness, and low self-esteem. They are not opposites, but two sides of the same coin. A penny is still a penny no matter which side is up. *I* is still the most important word."

To move beyond my fear of failure and start writing again, I didn't need to develop more self-love or work on improving my self-esteem. What I needed to do was to take my eyes off of me and put them on Christ in order to find freedom from my self-consciousness and fear of failure and criticism. Only from that place could I reach out and take risks, for it is in Christ's love, not my own, that I feel secure.

As I discussed in chapter 3, God gives each of us a measure of talents and abilities to be used for his kingdom. When we fail to use the gifts wisely or even deny we have them, we squander his good gifts. Even the apostle Paul felt inadequate in what the Lord had called him to, but his astute words remind us that our adequacy comes from Christ and not from ourselves (2 Corinthians 3:5). When God stretches us beyond our capabilities, he does it so that we might learn to depend on him and give him the glory. When we feel most feeble is not the time to shrink back and withdraw. It is the time to pray for a fresh opportunity to experience God's power—to tap the truth yet deeper still. Our weakness is not all about us and what we can or cannot do; it is about him and what he can do through us (Ephesians 2:10).

Fear of Rejection and Disapproval

Debbie was known as a servant. She toiled tirelessly, coordinating the church nursery and food pantry. She taught Sunday school and volunteered her help in the youth group. Never a week went by that Debbie wasn't involved in some sort of weeknight ministry at the church. People would often call her to help because everyone knew they could count on Debbie. She rarely said no. If she did, it was usually due to a scheduling conflict.

There is no question that Debbie is a hard worker, a servant of others. Again, these qualities characterize a humble heart. The question we must ask ourselves if we are like Debbie is *why* do we do what we do? For Debbie, her endless service was rooted in a fear of others' rejection or disapproval, not in the love of God. On the surface, her actions looked like a servant's, but her motives were self-centered. She was thinking of herself as she served others. Debbie loved the praise of people and knocked herself out so she wouldn't disappoint anyone. Instead of appearing selfish, she appeared sacrificial, but Debbie had no real freedom to stop and ask the Lord what he would have her do. She was too busy, wrapped up in her people-pleasing behaviors to give God much personal time.

Recently I was at a conference where a man was honored as a "real servant, an other-centered person." Everyone knew what that meant, but I'm afraid that sometimes we have been taught that to be godly, we must become other-centered. This is incorrect. God never teaches us to be other-centered; he tells us to be God-centered. When we put others at our center, our decisions will revolve around what they want so that they will like us, will want to be with us, or will not reject us. Paul wrote that the love of Christ is to "control" us (2 Corinthians 5:14, NASB). When we are ruled or controlled by the love of others or their lack of love for us, we are not God-centered.[3]

The fear of rejection or disapproval is not that different from the fear of failure. Rather than concentrating on our inadequacies or failures, we focus on what we must do to earn the acceptance or approval of someone we admire. The apostle Peter is easy to relate to because he struggled in so many of the same ways we do. During his ministry after Christ's death, Peter began to slip into an other-centered focus instead of staying God-centered. He feared the disapproval of the Jews. The apostle Paul saw Peter getting off track, and he severely rebuked him, even going so far as to call Peter a hypocrite (Galatians 2:11-14). John Bevere said, "If you desire the praise of man, you will fear man. If you fear man, you will serve him—for you will serve what you fear."[4] Whether in prideful self-centeredness or fearful self-consciousness, we all struggle with the temptation to put ourselves or others at our center instead of God. Authentic humility releases us from preoccupation with ourselves and with others' opinions of us.

I JUST WANT TO HIDE: THE PROBLEM WITH SHAME

Have you ever felt so awful inside you wanted to disappear? I'll never forget elementary school and how much I craved to be a part of the in-group. Recess was torture. Kids would stream out to the playground for a game of kickball. The two most popular girls would gather everyone around them and pick who they wanted on their team.

Rhonda started. "I'll take Susie," she said.

"Mary!" shouted the other team captain.

"Kathy's on my team," Rhonda crowed.

And on it went, back and forth until most of the girls were chosen for the teams. Bargaining came next for the players no one wanted. "I don't want Leslie," snipped Rhonda. "You take her."

"I don't want her either. She can't kick, but I'll take her if you give me Kathy and take Betty."

Back and forth this little ritual went until all the girls were either chosen or assigned. Those of us who were assigned knew our place. So did everyone else. No one really wanted us. Even retelling the story makes me recall the horrible shame I felt as a child.

Shame! This feeling deep within our being makes us want to hide, disappear, and sometimes even die. Shame makes us feel exposed and vulnerable. People whose opinions matter have declared us unworthy, imperfect, flawed, and we are undone—sometimes temporarily, sometimes more permanently.

Everyone experiences shame to some degree or another. As children we feel shame when we are the last to be picked for a team or when we are made fun of because someone saw us picking our nose. As adults we experience shame when our colleague tells us that our zipper is down, or when we have to stop to ask for directions because we're lost, or when we are confronted and forced to admit we're wrong. When no one notices that our nose needs wiping or our zipper is slipping, or sees our mistakes and failures, we usually don't feel shame; we just take care of the problem. But the knowing eye of another brings shame upon us. Feeling embarrassed, stupid, foolish, inadequate, or flawed are other ways to describe the experience of shame. It washes over us like a powerful wave and makes us want to hide from the person who sees, the person who knows.

Shame is part of being human. It reminds us of our limitations: We are not perfect; we are not God. Shame is slightly different from guilt in that guilt typically results from something we do (our behavior), while shame results from something we are or are not (our identity). Like guilt, shame can actually be a blessing when it helps us recognize our sin and limitations and feel our desperate need for God's love and grace. But more often, just like Adam and Eve when they realized their shame, it makes us want to hide.

Recently one of my clients asked me to write a letter to her employer on her behalf. I agreed and sent it off. Several weeks later she came into her session with a copy of my letter. She was thankful that I wrote it but pointed out to me that I had misspelled two words. I was filled with shame. Here I am, a college graduate and a writer, and I cannot spell. The shame wasn't in learning I misspelled some words. I already knew I was a lousy speller. The shame came because now she knew it too! I feared I would lose her respect.

For some people, shame is a way of life. They constantly feel afraid or exposed, defensive or intimidated. For these folks, shame not only defines them as imperfect or dependent creatures; it judges them worthless failures.

William was an attractive, bright thirty-year-old man who lived far beneath his potential. He never finished college and worked in a series of low-paying, dead-end jobs. He still lived with his elderly parents and was filled with bitterness and resentment. William's parents were overprotective of their only child. When he was in elementary school, they rarely allowed him to play with other children or get involved in sports. Today William feels like a failure, a wimp. "I should be stronger, more masculine, and more independent," William said. "Instead I feel weak, scared, and broken. I hate myself, but I don't know how to be any different."

This level of shame often leads to self-hatred. People filled with shame see themselves and everything that happens to them through the lens of *I knew you were never any good. Who could love you?* rather

than *God sees my flaws, my sins, my weaknesses and still loves me!*
William interpreted even small struggles in his life as a confirmation
that he was a loser. At first glance, people like William may appear
humble because they are self-effacing, but humility isn't weakness.
True humility requires inner strength to face the truth about ourselves
and to receive undeserved favor from a loving God who longs to rec-
oncile people to himself and help them grow.

I Cannot Forgive Myself: The Problem with Self-Hatred

Self-hatred also can occur when we fail ourselves. We are disappointed
that we have not lived up to our own ideals. Judy came to see me
because she was depressed. She was a professional woman and the
single parent of a teenager and a two-year-old son. By the time she
finally came for counseling, Judy felt suicidal and was filled with self-
hatred. As her story unfolded, I discovered that about three years
earlier Judy became pregnant out of wedlock. At the time of her pregnancy she was involved in the pro-life movement through her church.
Abortion was out of the question; she was repulsed at the thought of
it. Judy's pregnancy and delivery were difficult, but she gave birth to a
healthy baby boy and decided to raise him as a single parent. Three
months later, exhausted and overwhelmed, Judy discovered she was
pregnant again.

"I was so ashamed, Leslie. How could I have been so stupid? I'm
not a teenager. I know I shouldn't have been sexually active, but I
never dreamed I'd get pregnant so soon after the baby was born, especially because I was nursing."

"What happened next?" I asked.

"I panicked," Judy cried. "I couldn't go through another pregnancy."

Her doctor suggested she have an abortion, and in a moment of confusion and fear, she agreed.

"I can't believe I did such a horrible thing," Judy lamented. "I murdered my child. I will never forgive myself."

I tried to shift Judy's focus for a moment and offered, "God forgives sins, even big ones, Judy." But that truth provided no comfort to her. She would not forgive herself. Judy's suffering was not only from the guilt of killing her unborn child but from the shame of failing to live up to her own ideal of herself.

Judy's pain was heart-wrenching, her inner torment real. She had no problem identifying herself as a sinner or worse. But her self-hatred was not humility, it was wounded pride. Let's look a little more closely at some of the key statements Judy makes to reveal this subtle difference. She said, "How could I have been so stupid?" In Judy's eyes, she failed herself. She should somehow be above foolishness or stupid choices. Another statement exposed her wounded pride more fully when she cried, "I can't believe I did such a horrible thing." Judy believed she wasn't capable of such an awful act. Judy's behavior didn't shock God—he knew what she was capable of. It was Judy who was surprised.

Judy hated herself because she turned out to be less than she thought she was or expected herself to be. She was made small and ugly in her own eyes by her hasty decision to abort her unborn child. These truths about the darker side of herself were unacceptable to her. Her pervasive guilt and shame over what she had done grew into self-hatred.

In the Bible, Judas also experienced guilt and self-hatred when he betrayed Christ. Matthew tells us that Judas was "seized with remorse and returned the thirty silver coins to the chief priests and the elders." Judas exclaimed, "I have sinned...for I have betrayed innocent blood."

However, instead of seeking Christ's forgiveness and receiving his grace, he went out and hanged himself (Matthew 27:3-5).

All of us are tempted to turn to self-hatred instead of repentance when we fail to live up to our own standards. Our exposure shames us. Calvin Miller says, "Those who are easily depressed are usually those who were confident they could handle anything, until the gaseous bubble of their confidence was pricked by their failure. Their pride had set them up for the fall."[5]

When we see the true picture of who we are, we either turn toward self in disgust or toward Christ in humble repentance. Of course we hate our sin, but we recognize and accept that it is only by his grace and because of his love that he is willing to take away our guilt and shame.

Not too long ago I promised a colleague that we'd have lunch together during a professional conference we both attended. Later on in the morning I ran into an old friend who invited me to join her for lunch. Since I hadn't seen her in a long while, I agreed and went back and cancelled my luncheon plans with my other colleague. While my friend and I were eating lunch, I glanced up and saw my colleague eating all alone. His eyes met mine, and immediately I felt guilt and shame. *I should have invited him to join me and my friend,* I thought to myself, but then again, I knew why I hadn't. I wanted to enjoy my friend all by myself. My selfishness had won out at the expense of my colleague's feelings. Immediately I hated what I had done and was tempted to punish myself for my self-centeredness. But Jesus swiftly reminded me that he was already punished for my sin; I didn't need to inflict it upon myself. Instead, I needed to repent and humbly seek my colleague's forgiveness.

Self-hatred is the proud person's response to the failure to live up to his or her ideal. One person may say, "Look at me for what I have done," and it's called boasting. Another who is full of self-loathing declares, "How could I be capable of such an awful thing? I have failed to live up to what I expect of myself." One is relishing in vainglory; the other is mourning a wounded pride. Fénelon counseled, "Go forward always with confidence, without letting yourself be touched by the grief of a sensitive pride, which cannot bear to see itself imperfect."[6]

IT'S *NOT* ALL ABOUT ME!

The Lord continually reminds us that life is not oriented around us, our wants, our needs, or our desires. Nor does it revolve around our faults, our defects, or our weaknesses. Calvin Miller says, "We gain true humility not by putting ourselves down but by standing next to Christ."[7] Our natural tendency will always be to promote the self, defend the self, protect the self, and hide the self, all because we innately and naturally love ourselves much more than we love God or love others.

A life that is centered on self, whether it is in pursuit of pleasure or avoidance of pain, is not a life led by genuine humility. A heart swelling in pride or hiding in fear, will never be a heart that loves God completely and freely. It is a heart that loves self too much, and in the quest to gain more will lose it all.

Jesus shows us a different way altogether: the way of selflessness.

WHO SHALL DELIVER ME?

God strengthen me to bear myself;
That heaviest weight of all to bear,
Inalienable weight of care.

All others are outside myself;
I lock my door and bar them out,
The turmoil, tedium gad-about.

I lock my door upon myself,
And bar them out; but who shall wall
Self from myself, most loathed of all?

If I could once lay down myself,
And start self-purged upon the race
That all must run! Death runs apace.

If I could set aside myself,
And start with lightened heart upon
The road by all men overgone!

God harden me against myself,
This coward with pathetic voice
Who craves for ease, and rest, and joys:

Myself, arch-traitor to myself;
My hollowest friend, my deadliest foe,
My clog whatever road I go.

Yet One there is can curb myself,
Can roll the strangling load from me,
Break off the yoke and set me free.[8]

—Christina Rossetti

PERSONAL APPLICATION

Pick the area you struggle most with—excessive self-consciousness, shame, or self-hatred—and begin to confess it as sin instead of seeing it as low self-esteem. Perhaps you have been more focused on feeling bad about yourself rather than accepting yourself as an imperfect, flawed, and sinful person in need of God's strength, forgiveness, and grace. Journalize your thoughts and feelings about this, and write out a prayer to God asking him to help you make this mental and emotional shift in the way you see yourself. For example:

> *Dear God, I never saw some of my feelings as a problem with pride until now. I thought that I didn't think enough of myself, but I'm beginning to see that maybe I think way too much of myself and not enough about you. When I'm disappointed in myself, I continue to feel sad about me instead of finding acceptance and grace in you. Lord, I confess that I am too focused on me. Please teach me to take my eyes off myself and to put them on you. Show me how to see myself more truthfully and help my heart to trust you.*

Jesus: Our Example of Selflessness

The nothing believes itself something;

and the All-Powerful makes himself nothing.

FRANÇOIS FÉNELON

As a child, I always wanted to take piano lessons, but there was never enough money. After Howard and I were married, the first official piece of furniture we bought was a piano, and I began my long-sought-after lessons. I loved learning, and I even loved practicing. I thrilled at hearing my own fingers play such beautiful music. One day my teacher asked me to consider playing the offertory during church. I eagerly agreed and diligently prepared for the big day. It was a more difficult piece than I was used to, but I was anxious to show off my new talent by playing complicated chords and fancy runs. I was ready. I knew the music so well I could have played it blindfolded.

During my "performance" everything was going perfectly until I hit a wrong chord. I froze. My mind went blank, and try as I might, I could not find my place. Each attempt sounded more awful than the last, chords clashing, notes clanging, nothing like I had prepared. I ran from the service vowing never to play the piano in public again. The offering continued in marked silence. I was humiliated—but I was not humbled.

Caron, a friend of mine, told me a similar story with a much different ending. She said, "Many years ago I was a choir member in a large church. It was Christmastime, and I had been given a solo in the Christmas musical. At the first rehearsal, with the whole choir present, when my turn came to sing...to my horror...I froze. I had been singing for a number of years, and this had never happened to me. I was so embarrassed and undone by it that I spent several days in agony. During this time I realized how far I had wandered from my true focus of worship serving an audience of One. I decided to step aside from singing for a while, and it wasn't until several years later that I felt 'released' to sing publicly again. I didn't see this as a punishment but a time to let humility do its work in my heart. My time 'on the bench' was so effective that even years later, after I had moved into a role as full-time worship leader, I felt free from the problem of self-absorption. Now I'm asking God for a similar breakthrough in the areas of my writing and speaking—though I pray it doesn't require the same level of embarrassment!"

Humiliation Doesn't Always Lead to Learning Humility

Caron and I had similar experiences in which our failures shamed and humiliated us. But humiliation doesn't guarantee humility. It takes courage to be willing to allow humiliating experiences to teach us its lessons. Otherwise, these situations will only wound us, destroy us, or enrage us. They will reinforce our stubborn determination to withdraw in a self-protective posture or to go on the offensive, usually

by blaming or verbally attacking the person or situation that humiliated us.

After enduring many years of relentless verbal abuse from her husband, Sandy decided to seek some counsel on how to confront him.
With much prayer and consultation, she decided that she would ask
her pastor and another elder to come with her to help her speak with
her husband about his behavior and to provide her a measure of safety.
When confronted, Josh was furious that Sandy had spoken to out-
siders about family matters. "How dare you come to my home and
talk to me that way!" he screamed. Josh was humiliated. His sin was
exposed, but instead of humbling himself and repenting, Josh was
enraged. He accused the pastor of meddling, blamed Sandy for not
being submissive, and broke off his friendship with the elder.

One of the reasons why we find joy and humility so difficult to
connect is because when we recall our most humiliating experiences,
we remember that we felt dreadful and horrified, not joyful or satisfied. Yet, as Caron suggests, as we learn to humble ourselves and find
freedom from our pride, self-absorption, or self-protectiveness, we
find joy and happiness in becoming who God has made us, and in loving and serving God and others. Why? Because we're finally beginning
to grasp—it is *not* all about us!

JESUS TEACHES US HUMILITY

My husband, Howard, coaches Junior Olympics girls' volleyball. He
is passionate about the sport and is a good teacher. He patiently pours
hours into showing girls the fundamental skills of the game and how
to execute those skills well. Every so often he gets frustrated when one
of his players thinks that she knows better than he does how to perform the skills and refuses to submit to his instruction. It makes him

sad, he says, because, "Her pride keeps her from becoming an excellent player. She refuses to be taught. She thinks she knows it all already."

I wonder if Jesus would say that about us sometimes. "Leslie, you will not grow or become the person I have created you to be, because you will not allow me to teach you my ways. You think you know it all already." Our pride will always keep us from maturing into the person God has designed us to be. Humility is essential for intimacy with God and foundational for any spiritual growth and maturity to take place.

Learning from Christ is a lifetime walk in his school of holiness. Jesus invites us, "Come to me, all you who are weary and burdened, and I will give you rest. Take my yoke upon you and learn from me, for I am gentle and humble in heart, and *you will find rest for your souls.* For my yoke is easy and my burden is light" (Matthew 11:28-30, emphasis added).

Are you willing?

Jesus Chose Humility

God's Word teaches us that the essence of the Christian walk is to become more and more like Christ, both in our outward and inner lives (Romans 8:29). Jesus had plenty of humiliating experiences, as when he was stripped of his clothes and mocked and beaten (Mark 15:16-20), but these things did not make Christ humble. Jesus was humble because he *chose* to be humble. The apostle Paul wrote: "Your attitude should be the same as that of Christ Jesus: Who, being in very nature God, did not consider equality with God something to be grasped, but *made himself* nothing, taking the very nature of a servant, being made in human likeness. And being found in appearance as a man, *he humbled himself* and became obedient to death—even death on a cross!" (Philippians 2:5-8, emphasis added).

Many years ago I was speaking with a minister who was in the midst of preparing his Easter sermon. He called it "The Great Tragedy." Curious, I asked him what it was about. He replied, "Christ's death was the great tragedy. What might he have become if the Jews hadn't killed him?"

I thought to myself, *No one took Christ's life*. Jesus gave his life because of his great love for his Father. There wasn't anything Jesus would rather do than glorify his Father—even if that meant his death.

The birth pangs of humility commence when we not only acknowledge the truth about ourselves but emotionally accept it as well. No one can make us humble, although God may orchestrate some humiliating experiences to help us recognize our need for humility. (For an example of this, see Daniel 4–5.) As Christians, we readily agree that we need God for salvation, but it is much harder to really believe that we need him for everything.

The previous passage from Philippians tells us that Jesus humbled himself and made himself nothing. The word *humbled* used in the Greek language means "to make low." We can be humiliated by plenty of people and a myriad of experiences, but as we have seen, authentic humility begins when we choose to lower ourselves and embrace the truth about who we are. Jesus knew that in addition to being the very essence of God, he became human through the Incarnation. Jesus willingly limited himself when he was born in a physical body. Jesus was never forced to be humble; out of reverence for God, he lowered himself.

Jesus continued to humble himself when he lived his life in total dependence upon God the Father for meaning and purpose. Perhaps that is why he spent so much time in prayer. He sought his Father's presence, provision, and direction so that he would see reality clearly and not become disoriented or distracted by temporal things. Jesus continually affirmed that he was not here to serve himself but to serve his Father and glorify him (see John 5:19,30; 7:28; 8:50). Jesus not only acknowledged his dependency upon God, he lived it out in every word he spoke, every step he took, and every decision he made. Jesus modeled to us how we are to relate to God. When we become that mindful of our position, our purpose, and our neediness, we, too, will humble ourselves.

One winter day my husband and I hit the ski slopes. I've never been a great or daring skier but often enjoyed (past tense) skiing on the beginner to intermediate slopes at a ski resort not too far from our home. Once a wrong turn (or bad advice) led us to the top of Diamond Head, the advanced slope, which was filled with icy moguls and steep curves. It was bitter cold, and as I tentatively started skiing down the treacherous mountain, I was sure I was going to die. Howard (who is a much better skier than I) tried to coach me along, but I was so afraid I started sobbing uncontrollably. "I can't do it," I wailed. No sooner had the words left my mouth than my eyes beheld the sweetest sight I'd seen all day—a ski patrol instructor whizzing by on his snowmobile. "HELP!!!" I shouted at the top of my lungs. As he stopped, I begged him to let me ride on the back of his mechanical white horse, convincing him that if he didn't rescue me then, he'd have to come back for an injured or dead person later. My need was ever so great that I readily humbled myself before the ski instructor.

Perhaps you might be thinking, *What was courageous about calling for help? It would have been braver to try to ski down the mountain.* Our pride is slippery and most deceptive. We don't want to see or admit that we are desperate people. We'd rather believe that we can maneuver life's twists and turns all by ourselves and come through unscathed. Our pride and our stubbornness deceive us into believing that we can have an effective and productive life without surrendering ourselves to the one who created us.

That is not the truth. Jeremiah lamented, "But these people have stubborn and rebellious hearts; they have turned aside and gone away. They do not say to themselves, 'Let us fear the LORD our God, who gives autumn and spring rains in season, who assures us of the regular weeks of harvest.' Your wrongdoings have kept these away; your sins have deprived you of good" (Jeremiah 5:23-25). How bold of us to think we can live for even one minute without the provision and benevolence of God. It's like a two-year-old thinking that he doesn't need his parents. How absurd. It takes far more courage to face ourselves honestly and admit our weakness and our neediness than to continue in arrogant self-deception.

Jesus' life demonstrated a total absence of pride. Where pride is, humility cannot be. They cannot coexist in the same heart. Jesus knew that his entire being was fully dependent upon God. He did not live his life for his own glory or to meet his own felt needs. He knew that keeping the Father in first place was absolutely essential to fulfilling his purpose, and he understood how wonderfully worthy the Father was of his undivided devotion and attention.

Perhaps more than any other virtue, humility causes us to begin to resemble Jesus. Yet everything in us resists this lowering of ourselves. We want to make ourselves big and God small. But God, who is strong, made himself weak so that he might make us, who are weak, strong through him. James said, "Humble yourselves before the Lord, and he will lift you up" (James 4:10). Peter said, "Clothe yourselves with humility toward one another, because, 'God opposes the proud but gives grace to the humble'" (1 Peter 5:5). Humility can only start to do its work in our hearts and lives when we *choose* its path.

Jesus Submitted Himself to God

Humble-mindedness must eventually become humble-heartedness if it is to do its work in our lives. Jesus yielded himself to God, totally and completely. That doesn't mean he never questioned God; it means he never challenged him or argued with him. After Jesus was arrested, the soldiers beat him, stripped him of his clothes, and spit on him, and then with utter contempt they mocked the Son of God with their feigned worship and belittling words. How tempting it must have been for Jesus to prove himself Deity, to defend himself and silence those ignorant mockers with his angelic army. Yet he chose not to. Such a move would have thwarted God's plan. Jesus fully believed that God knew best, and he only wanted to do what the Father wanted him to do, even when it was excruciatingly painful. In some of Christ's recorded prayers, we see him humbly submitting himself to God's perfect will (see Matthew 26:42; John 12:27-28), and in the Lord's Prayer, he teaches us to do likewise (Matthew 6:9-13).

When we believe that submitting to God will cause us to miss out on something vital to our well-being, we have been deceived by pride. Jeff got caught in that lie. His marriage was shaky, and he was vulnerable. A coworker began to give him attention, and it felt like cool water to a parched throat. Jeff knew that God says adultery is wrong, but he felt so empty and so lonely. God wasn't meeting his felt needs. His wife was distant, and this woman was available. Like forbidden fruit, she appeared necessary to his life and happiness. Jeff faced a crossroads. Would he try to fill the emptiness in his life with temporal pleasure, or would he find the courage to walk a different path and learn to trust God in a deeper way?

Jesus faced the same temptations that we do, yet he never faltered (Hebrews 4:15). When Christ was in the desert following his forty-day fast, Satan tried to deceive him using his age-old plan of cleverly twisting the truth (see Matthew 4:1-11). Satan's first offensive strategy was to get Jesus to focus on himself and his felt needs. "If you are the Son of God, tell these stones to become bread," Satan taunted. The issue at stake wasn't whether Jesus was the Son of God; Satan knew that he was. Satan hoped to distract Christ by getting him to prove it, to do miracles for his own glory, and to meet his own needs instead of yielding himself to God. Satan wasn't simply tempting Jesus to make bread because he was hungry; Satan was tempting Jesus to go his own way (pride) and to satisfy himself (independence from God). Satan's subsequent challenges and Jesus' response to those temptations clearly show us that Christ was centered on one thing: His only interest was in doing what God wanted him to do.

Jeff was tempted by the thought that he would find happiness and joy apart from God and his ways. That is the lie that Eve fell for in the garden (see Genesis 3), and it is the same lie that we must all guard our heart against today. Jesus shows us something radically different— steadfast obedience generated from a humble heart. Andrew Murray says, "Jesus found this life of entire self-abnegation, of absolute submission and dependence upon the Father's will, to be one of perfect peace and joy. He lost nothing by giving all to God."[1]

Jesus Served Others

If anyone deserved to be served it was Jesus. After all, he was God's Son, the Messiah, the King of kings, and Lord of lords. The angels would have joyfully ministered to Christ day and night. But throughout Jesus' life and ministry, he identified himself as a servant, not a superstar (Matthew 20:28).

Most of us find it difficult to be a true servant, especially an unrecognized or unappreciated servant. We may do nice or helpful things for others and for God, but it is often with the worldly mind-set of "What's in it for me?" At the very least, we want those whom we serve to notice, appreciate our efforts, or give something back to us. Then our service becomes servility, and we lose the joy-filled blessing of servanthood. All of us who are married or have children get some practice in learning true servanthood, though we often fail to embrace the humility that Christ is trying to develop in us through these family relationships.

Casey's marriage was in trouble. Her husband, Joe, was drifting further and further away from her. Armed with some tips on how to be a good Christian wife, Casey embarked on a mission to save her marriage. She made nice dinners, ironed Joe's shirts without his having to ask, and daily cleaned the house. She stopped criticizing him and complaining about how little money he earned. After about two months, Casey gave up. "It's not working," she cried. "I've tried everything to make our marriage better and to get him to respond positively, but nothing helps." Casey's actions may have resembled servanthood, but her hidden agenda made them mere servility. In truth, her acts of service were not for her husband but for herself. Casey served her husband as a strategy to get him to change and care for her. Please don't misunderstand; the things Casey desired from her husband weren't sinful, nor was she wrong for wanting to improve their relationship. However, genuine servanthood comes from a heart that is emptied of self-serving agendas. In humble service, obedience to God is paramount—there are no strings attached.

Jesus modeled servanthood throughout his ministry on earth, but the most poignant example he left us was that of washing the feet of his disciples (John 13:1-17). He did this to show his disciples love in action. He wanted them to know that understanding something intellectually and actually acting on that understanding are two different things. When I learned counseling theory in graduate school, I had no problem conceptually. I was a good student and easily excelled. However, applying those nice theories to hurting people in their life's difficulties was a new challenge altogether. I found at first that what I knew in my head was not easily applied to real life.

Many of us know our faith intellectually; it is information we collect. Jesus challenges our academic head knowledge to mature into heartfelt faith in action. Up to now we have learned that we should be humble and loving. We know we shouldn't be selfish or self-centered, but actually humbling ourselves is much harder than merely agreeing to the concept. Selfless servanthood takes specific action, and humble actions are only possible when we first humble ourselves before God. As we do this, then God's grace enables us to humble ourselves before others and become their servant. As we willingly and humbly yield ourselves to God's authority, he will empower us to serve him by submitting to and serving others, however or wherever he calls us to do so.

Biblical examples of foot washing also teach us how to receive—to humble ourselves and recognize our need to be tended to. Jesus allowed a woman of ill repute to wash his feet with her tears and tenderly wipe them with her hair as she poured costly perfume on them (Luke 7:36-39). As I read that story with fresh eyes, I felt sad. The Lord brought to mind the times I refused to allow others to minister to me, especially those I deemed less fortunate. I could serve them, but I would not allow them to serve me. I acted as if I had no needs.

Because of my pride and self-sufficiency, I have missed out on some of the blessings God wanted to give me. In the process of receiving another's gift of service, we have the opportunity to learn more about our neediness and to experience grace—unmerited favor.

There are those who would rather eat cold canned soup than allow a neighbor to bring them a meal. We feel uncomfortable when someone from church offers to clean our home when we've been ill or hands us some cash when we've been out of work. We don't want others to be privy to our neediness, to our weakness. When Peter refused to allow Christ to wash his feet, Christ corrected this attitude in him. Rather than feel humbled and thankful for someone's kindness toward us, our pride shuns help or keeps score by returning the favors. Jesus' foot-washing experiences demonstrate humility in action, both as the one who graciously serves and the one who graciously receives.

What Humility Looks Like

Jesus was the best kind of teacher. He lived what he taught and often illustrated his lessons through story or metaphor so that those who had ears to hear would more fully grasp the importance of his teachings. Jesus not only modeled selflessness through his own life, but he taught us that in order to become more and more like him we, too, must learn to humble ourselves, yield more fully to God, and unselfishly serve others.

The Secret of Servant Leadership

We live in a me-first world that values power and recognition. Our culture adores superstars. Every mother dreams that her child will become someone important, someone significant. In Jesus' day it wasn't all that different. The mother of James and John, two of Christ's disciples, asked Jesus to grant her sons the best seats in his kingdom, each sitting alongside Jesus, one to his right and the other to his left. Jesus used this moment to tell his disciples about a different way of being great. He said, "Whoever wants to become great among you must be your servant, and whoever wants to be first must be your slave—just as the Son of Man did not come to be served, but to serve, and to give his life as a ransom for many" (Matthew 20:26-28).

Taking our place as a servant doesn't necessarily mean that those who have high positions or are recognized as leaders should step down or are sinning. However, Jesus cautions those who do have seats of honor and authority or who have power over others against misusing those God-ordained positions for self-centered purposes (Matthew 20:25-26). Those roles are given to us by God to humbly serve the individuals or groups entrusted to our care. Francis de Sales warns, "The King of Glory does not reward his servants according to the dignity of the offices they hold but according to the love and humility with which they fulfill their offices."[2]

Frank demanded unwavering obedience from his wife, Joan, and their three children. Anytime Joan expressed a differing opinion or concern over his harsh treatment of the children, Frank berated her for not being submissive to his authority as her husband. Tension pulsated throughout the home as everyone walked on eggshells. Tired of pleading to be heard and understood, Joan sighed and said, "It's Frank's way or it's no way. I guess I'm supposed to submit to him because God says he's the head of our home."

It's unfortunate that many husbands have used their God-given position in their homes for selfish purposes. They believe that being the head gives them license to do or demand anything they want and that their wives are supposed to comply and be submissive. This ought not to be. Jesus rebuked the Pharisees because of their self-serving, self-centered leadership. Jesus cautioned his disciples not to misuse their authority as the rulers of the Gentiles did (see Matthew 20:25; Ephesians 5:25-33). Christ teaches us a radically different kind of leadership—servant leadership.

Humility gives us a proper lens through which to view ourselves. It protects us against using our status, authority, and power for selfish purposes. Embracing humility reminds us that we are not better than anyone else and that people are not to be used to feed our egos or make us happy. If we have been given a position of leadership, whether it be in our church, our community, or our home, humility teaches us that we are to use those positions to minister to others and to please God. As we yield ourselves in humble service for others, God says that he will exalt us (Matthew 23:12).

The Secret of Smallness

One way Jesus taught his followers more about humility was to compare it to the attitude of a small child. Jesus said, "I tell you the truth, unless you change and become like little children, you will never enter the kingdom of heaven. Therefore, whoever humbles himself like this child is the greatest in the kingdom of heaven" (Matthew 18:3-4). Jesus doesn't mean that we should stay immature or childish, but that we should recognize our smallness relative to God's greatness.

When my children were little, our family would buy a season pass to a large amusement park near our home. It was a kid's paradise. One side of the park was packed with rides like roller coasters, Ferris wheels, carousels, and bumper cars, and the other side hosted a gigantic wave pool, water slides, tubing, and other water attractions. On a hot summer day, we would head out early to beat the crowds. The children loved to swim in the wave pool, bobbing and diving with the mechanical surf. But they would never go in alone. My daughter would tug at me, saying, "Mommy, come in with me. I'm too little to go in by myself." She felt no shame in confessing her smallness, just an honest awareness of herself and her need.

Saul felt small when God chose him to be Israel's first king. He replied to Samuel the prophet, "But am I not a Benjamite, from the smallest tribe of Israel, and is not my clan the least of all the clans of the tribe of Benjamin? Why do you say such a thing to me?" (1 Samuel 9:21). Saul knew his origins and humbled himself before Samuel and before God. After Saul became king, however, he became proud. He began to make decisions on his own and lied to Samuel about following the Lord's instructions. Finally Samuel confronted King Saul's deception. He said, "Stop! Let me tell you what the LORD said to me last night. *Although you were once small in your own eyes,* did you not become the head of the tribes of Israel?" (see 1 Samuel 15:16-17, emphasis added). Saul *was* small in his own eyes—but something changed. His heart had grown proud.

King Saul's pride problem is a battle we all face. Although we may initially recognize our smallness and humble ourselves, we can easily become puffed up by the admiration of others or with our own accomplishments. We start to think that everything is all about us and that God is lucky to have us on his side. Like King Saul, we begin to lean on our own understanding or our own way of doing things instead of surrendering ourselves to God's wisdom and his path for life. Jesus uses the posture of a child to help us understand how crucial humility is to our welfare. Jesus knows that if we forget our smallness, we will lose our way in our journey through life.

In addition to recognizing their limitations, small children usually believe that their parents know best. One summer my daughter,

Amanda, suffered a serious dog bite. Large teeth marks left their jagged imprint in her cheek, and we rushed her to the hospital. Hysterical, she wanted to go home. She didn't want stitches. She said she was fine. But as her parents, we knew that she needed a plastic surgeon to prevent her face from being permanently disfigured. Amanda didn't like it, but she yielded herself to our wisdom. She trusted that we loved her and would only act in her best interests. Today, at twenty years old, she is glad we overruled her protests and got her the stitches she needed. Jesus knows that humility is foundational to trusting God. He wants us to deeply believe that even when we don't understand or when life is hard, like a small child, we can safely tuck our hand into the hand of our heavenly Father and feel secure, trusting that he loves us and knows what is best for us.

So how do we start to empty ourselves of the idolatry of self so that we might become more like Christ and more fully surrendered to God? There is only way: Revere God.

PERSONAL APPLICATION

The Lord's Prayer (Matthew 6:9-13) is a perfect example of Christ's humility. Jesus begins his prayer in the position of a child, bowing himself to his Father's authority: "Our Father in heaven, hallowed be your name." Christ continues his submissive posture, yielding himself to his Father's authority and perfect will: "Your kingdom come, your will be done on earth as it is in heaven." Jesus then begins his petition, acknowledging his needs and his dependence upon his Father: "Give us today our daily bread. Forgive us our debts, as we also have forgiven our debtors, and lead us not into temptation, but deliver us from the evil one."

Begin to pray from the position of a child, humbly talking to God. Confess your neediness, your sinfulness, your dependence upon him. Praise God for his wisdom, his power, and his loving-kindness. Submit yourself to him, and ask him to deliver you from the temptation to exalt yourself, making yourself bigger than you really are.

The Fear of God Leads to Humility

The true way to be humble is not to stoop until you are
smaller than yourself, but to stand at your real height
against some higher nature that will show you
what the real smallness of your greatness is.

PHILLIPS BROOKS

When my daughter, Amanda, was in first grade, the teacher
sent home a note recommending that we get her eyes tested.
She was having trouble reading the board. After her examination, the
doctor invited me in.

"Amanda, read the letters on the wall for your mom," he said.

"What letters?" she replied. I stared at the wall with the large
alphabet hanging plain as day. She couldn't even see the largest E.
Then with a click of the lens, everything changed.

"Now can you read it, Amanda?"

"Oh that's easy," she chirped. "E, B, A, O, C, P, Q."

Amanda loved her glasses. They gave her the freedom to see the
world properly. Without them, she would not only have failed aca-
demically, she would not have been able to cross the street safely, ride
a bike, or even pick out matching clothes to wear. Just as Amanda

couldn't see without the help of corrective lenses, God tells us that we need spiritual lenses in order to correct our perspective and to see what really brings us lasting joy in life. He tells us that, without these spiritual lenses, we are blind and prone to being deceived and misled.

The Bible, God's Word, functions as our corrective lens so that we will view life accurately and live to our fullest potential. Yet many people don't take the time to read God's Word, or if they do, don't really believe it. Other things seem much more vital to our well-being than knowing and obeying God's Word. What does it mean when I scour the latest beauty magazine to discover how to get rid of my wrinkles but devote less time to searching the Scriptures to acquire inner beauty?

Today we are busy people chasing what we think we need to make life meaningful and productive. We spend an hour perusing and answering our e-mail but can't seem to find the time to listen to and talk with God. We wouldn't miss reading the daily newspaper but can't squeeze out precious moments to ponder or study the Scripture. We schedule our days, weeks, and months on our Palm Pilots or Day-Timers and prioritize those things we deem most worthy of our time and attention. Time spent with God is often on the B list—"Things to do when I get around to it." Oswald Chambers lamented, "We do not consciously disobey God, we simply do not heed Him. God has given us His commands; there they are, but we do not pay any attention to them, not because of wilful disobedience but because we do not love and respect Him."[1]

The *Wall Street Journal* is standard reading in the business world. It is filled with tips and strategies to make your business successful and your money grow. Followers base much of their business planning and investment strategies on the advice of this popular newspaper. Why?

Because they value and respect the experts who write it and believe that following their advice will lead to success.

Before we will take the Bible seriously as the corrective lens we so desperately need if we want to see life correctly, both now and eternally, we must first come to value and trust the One who authored it.

Let's take a closer look at God so that we will come to value and respect him as the only One who has the answer to discovering a deep and abiding joy in life. A. W. Tozer reminds us, "You can't make God big. But you can *see* Him big."[2] The way we view God does not change God, but it changes us and how we relate to him.

"He will be the sure foundation for your times, a rich store of salvation and wisdom and knowledge; *the fear of the LORD is the key to this treasure*" (Isaiah 33:6, emphasis added).

WHAT IS THE FEAR OF THE LORD?

I used to think that mature Christians weren't supposed to fear God. After all, how could we approach God as our Abba Father if we were afraid of him? When we're scared of someone, it's hard to imagine ourselves in a loving and intimate relationship with that person. Yet God longs for us to be in a trusting and loving relationship with him, so how can we love him and fear him at the same time?

When the Bible speaks of having the fear of God, it is describing something greater than simply being afraid of God. The Hebrew and Greek words for *fear* that are used in the original languages include not only being frightened of God's judgment or wrath, but having a holy reverence, an awe of God that goes beyond the terror of displeasing him. Fearing God properly inspires us and actually draws us toward him. When we fear God, we want to know him better, to serve him, and to please him by our lives.

The Bible tells us that unrepentant sinners should be afraid of God (see Hebrews 10:31), but Jesus and angelic beings, who are sinless, also fear him (see Psalm 89:7; Isaiah 11:1-3). Convinced that God alone is worthy of their undivided attention, they give him their deepest devotion. They are not afraid of his wrath; rather, they are awed and delighted by his presence. They are most deeply impressed by who he is: holy, omnipotent, omniscient, the Creator, our lover, and Lord of all. They fear the loss of his presence rather than the wrath of his presence.

If we're honest, most of us have to admit that we don't experience God as the one who most impresses us. Bill Gates or Billy Joel, Oprah Winfrey, Michael J. Fox, or perhaps George W. Bush might stand a better chance of grabbing our attention. We are awed by their power and personality or talent and would love to know a few of their secrets. We'd jump at the chance to meet them and would be honored if they invited us into their inner circle to know them more intimately.

Last year Cynthia Heald spoke at a women's conference in my area. I had the opportunity to have dinner with Cynthia and to drive her to the airport afterward. I relished this chance to have uninterrupted private time with this much-loved and respected Bible teacher and author. I was eager to learn all I could in our short time together. Afterward I asked myself whether I look forward to talking with God as much I looked forward to talking with Cynthia. Do I carve out special time in my hectic schedule to meet with God because I am so deeply taken with who he is that I can't wait to spend time with him and to know him better? Henry Nouwen challenges us when he says that if we really love God, we should be able to spend at least one hour a day with him alone. He wrote, "The question as to whether it is helpful, useful, practical, or fruitful is completely irrelevant, since the only reason to love is love itself. Everything else is secondary."[3]

The cornerstone of faith is a high esteem of almighty God. Only in revering God—in gaining a healthy fear of the Lord—will we find the keys to wisdom. Life is found in him, not in us (Acts 17:25).

Come, then, and see why we must grow more and more "deeply impressed" with God and less enamored with the world and ourselves if we want to find the abiding joy God speaks of.

The Greatness of God

Creation alone speaks enough about who God is that we ought to catch our breath in wonder and worship (Romans 1:20). Who else can set the stars, the sun, and planets into the universe in exactly the right spot so that we neither burn up nor freeze? The psalmist, awed by the beauty of God's handiwork, wrote, "The heavens declare the glory of God; the skies proclaim the work of his hands. Day after day they pour forth speech; night after night they display knowledge" (Psalm 19:1-2). And also, "When I consider your heavens, the work of your fingers, the moon and the stars, which you have set in place, what is man that you are mindful of him, the son of man that you care for him?" (Psalm 8:3-4). Not only are there billions of stars in our Milky Way galaxy, "Scientists estimate there are billions of galaxies, each of them loaded with billions of stars."[4] The psalmist proclaimed, "He determines the number of the stars and calls them each by name." No wonder he exclaimed, "Great is our Lord and mighty in power; his understanding has no limit" (Psalm 147:4-5).

Gazing at the heavens is one way to begin to get a sense of God's greatness and our smallness. The earth also manifests the hand of almighty God. One summer vacation, my family visited Bar Harbor off the coast of Maine. One of our more eventful day trips was a whale watch. My husband and kids describe it as one of the worst days of their lives. The seas were choppy, and the boat lurched up and down while cold, salty air whipped our faces. I loved it and felt like I was on a perpetual roller coaster. However, Howard was not happy. He was slumped over the rail the entire time, valiantly trying not to lose his breakfast. My children were sprawled on the deck below, clutching their stomachs. They felt small and powerless against the restless sea. Spellbound, I, too, felt small as I witnessed greatness, mystery, and beauty as whales danced in the ocean in the most marvelous ballet I had ever seen.

On another family trip, this one much more sedate, we visited the Baltimore Aquarium. We learned that the tropical rain forest contains more species of plants and animals than in all the rest of the world's ecosystems combined. Just one tree was home to forty-three different species of ants. My children's favorite exhibit was the poisonous frogs. Behind thick glass in tiny aquarium-like settings, these frogs were so beautiful they looked like expensive glass jewels. One miniature frog was clothed with lime green skin, and another was painted bright orange. Both sported black spots and poisonous tongues. Their beauty was dazzling yet so deeply tucked in the rain forest, who would ever see it? God—the One who created little jewel-toned frogs for his own pleasure.

While snorkeling in Mexico, I had a similar experience. An artist couldn't have painted fish to look more colorful and breathtaking. Whether we enjoy the sky streaked with purple and gold as the sun sets behind the mountains or the ocean shimmering the reflection of the sun, the frogs in the rain forest or the heavens twinkling with delight, all are made to impress us with the greatness and majesty of our God. The Bible tells us "the whole earth is full of his glory" (Isaiah 6:3). "Come, let us bow down in worship, let us kneel before the

LORD our Maker; for he is our God and we are the people of his pasture, the flock under his care" (Psalm 95:6-7).

God's magnificent creative works should move us to worship and revere him with deep humility. Unfortunately, many will acknowledge their smallness but will not bow to God's greatness. Carl Sagan, one of America's most renowned astronomers and astrophysicists, remained a steadfast atheist even as he approached his own death. A. W. Tozer suggested that "the modern scientist has lost God amid the wonders of His world."[5]

The Miracles of God

God is not only great; he is powerful. He does amazing things. You would think that we humans would be impressed with a God who could turn water into blood, split the seas in half, and make the sun stand still. According to the Old Testament, the people of Israel were impressed, but only temporarily. When the miraculous returned to the mundane, Israel soon forgot God. Time after time, God wooed Israel with his miraculous works by feeding them manna, bringing forth gushing water from a dusty desert rock, or leading them from within a cloud during the day and a pillar of fire by night. And time after time, Israel forgot God and started longing for idols. The psalmist laments, "They did not remember his power—the day he redeemed them from the oppressor, the day he displayed his miraculous signs in Egypt, his wonders in the region of Zoan" (Psalm 78:42-43).

When Jesus walked the earth, he healed the sick, miraculously fed the multitudes, and turned water into wine. And, as in the Old Testament, most were impressed, but not everyone believed. Even fewer worshiped him. I can't imagine a greater miracle than witnessing someone being raised from the dead. When Jesus called Lazarus to life, the dead man walked from his tomb still wrapped up tight in his grave clothes (John 11:38-44). What a frightening and awesome scene that must have been. Picture it today. The funeral is over, everyone is at the cemetery, red-eyed, waiting for the final lowering of the casket into the earth when someone shouts, "Stop! Larry, come out!" All of a sudden the casket lid creaks open, and fingers start curling around the edge of the casket rim. Hearts pound, and everyone's breathing momentarily stops as the body lifts itself from its wooden tomb. We'd feel terrified, but would it lead us to kneel at the feet of the one who possessed such power to raise the dead? Or would we be like the religious leaders who sought to have Jesus killed?

Early on in my Christian life I was desperate to see some real miracles. I thought my faith would grow if I could see the hand of God in an obvious display of his power. But as I read the accounts in Scripture, I saw that most people who were witnesses to the miraculous didn't deepen their relationship with Jesus. They enjoyed the blessings of the extra wine at the wedding or the food on the mountaintop or the healing touch of Christ, but they, too, soon forgot, returning to their everyday life.

The miraculous may cause us to take notice and to recognize the greatness behind the one who displays such powers, but as the Scriptures attest, it doesn't always lead us to bow in gratitude and reverent worship.

The Mystery of God

I am always a bit leery around people who believe they have God all figured out. They know the answers to all of life's complications and have simplistic explanations for troubling situations. I believe God is impressive but not always understandable. When we try to explain him, we reduce him to something we can grasp. That amounts to refashioning God according to our likeness. It is the height of pride to think that our human, finite brain can comprehend the mysteries of God or totally grasp his essence.

Job's friends had a simplistic approach to life. They could easily explain almost everything. Their philosophy went something like this: If you do good things, God makes you happy and blesses your life. If you are not happy or not having a good life, then that must mean you have done something wrong. Change what you're doing wrong, and all will be well. (The book of Job tells the story.)

Today some of us have the same view. "Why does a loving God allow bad things to happen to his children?" Donna sobbed. Her husband had been arrested for raping a college coed not too far from their apartment. He was caught close to the scene and positively identified by his victim. I said nothing. I didn't know how to respond as there was no simple answer.

"I don't understand," Donna lamented. "I did all the right things. This isn't supposed to happen to people like me. I went to a Christian college and was careful who I dated. My husband comes from a good home, and we were planning to be in full-time Christian service as soon as we paid off our college loans. We never even had sex before we got married! It is so unfair! Why would God let me choose someone who was capable of this horrendous act? My parents prayed for the person I would marry ever since I was born."

We don't like it when the cruelties of life cast dark shadows on the character of the Almighty and we can't explain or defend him. Donna wasn't wrong for asking her questions. Job, too, questioned God when he went through all his troubles, but God doesn't always explain himself to us in the way we might want him to. Even if he did, do you think we could always comprehend his explanation? "Who has understood the mind of the LORD, or instructed him as his counselor?" (Isaiah 40:13).

Parents can relate to this concept in part when our children ask us, "Why?" When my three-year-old asked, "Why do I have to go to the dentist if my teeth don't hurt?" was there any explanation I could give her that she would understand and accept? My usual approach when she was that age was to reply simply, "Because I said so," or, "Because it's important to get your teeth checked." Period. No further discussion. I knew she would not grasp the reason—it was beyond her understanding. But even as my children got older and I tried to explain things to them, oftentimes they couldn't or wouldn't get it. Often it was because they couldn't grasp the bigger picture; they lived in the present. Our desire as parents in those moments is that our children simply trust us to do them good, even when they don't understand.

At times we demand that God explain things to us. Life is painful, and we don't get it. God sometimes answers us as I did my daughter: "Because it's good for you," or, "Because I said so." He wants us to be like a child and simply trust him. But often we don't. We want an explanation we can understand. We think he owes us that much. Sometimes God does clarify things for us, and often as we spiritually mature, his ways make more sense. Other times, God may answer our questions in ways we don't expect.

Instead of responding to Job's demand for answers, God asked Job some questions of his own. God began with, "Where were you when I laid the earth's foundation?" (Job 38:4) and, "Have you ever given orders to the morning, or shown the dawn its place, that it might take

the earth by the edges and shake the wicked out of it?" (verses 12-13).
God's probing of Job continued. "Have the gates of death been shown
to you?" (verse 17) and, "Have you comprehended the vast expanses
of the earth? Tell me if you know all this.... Do you know the laws of
the heavens? Can you set up God's dominion over the earth?" (verses
18,33). God relentlessly challenged Job with more than fifty questions
and ended round one with this finale: "Will the one who contends
with the Almighty correct him?" (40:2).

How many times do we try to correct God? *I think you made a
mistake here, God. This wasn't supposed to happen this way. God, what
were you thinking when you let this take place? If I were in charge, I
would have done it this other way instead.*

Job did not get angry at God for not giving him the answers he
wanted or for not fixing his problems. Instead, Job humbled himself
and repented. He said, "I am unworthy—how can I reply to you? I
put my hand over my mouth" (40:4). Sensing God's magnificence and
majesty and mystery silenced Job. His heightened awareness caused
him to see someone greater than himself or his troubles. Later on, after
another round of questions, Job further responded to God's mysterious ways in humble worship: "Surely I spoke of things I did not understand, things too wonderful for me to know" (42:3).

Sometimes we try to make God small in order to explain him. In
the process, we lose our appreciation for the mystery of God. His ways
are beyond our ability to grasp fully or to know completely. A. W.
Tozer wrote, "The believing man does not claim to understand.
He falls to his knees and whispers, 'God.' The man of earth kneels
also, but not to worship. He kneels to examine, to search, to find the
cause and the how of things.... We are more likely to explain than to
adore."[6]

The Loving-Kindness of God

Most people picture God mighty and powerful. We acquiesce that his ways might be a bit beyond our human finite understanding. Indeed, if he is truly God, they must be, or we would be his equal. The greatest mystery of all, the thing that pierces our pride like a pin bursts a boil, is God's loving-kindness toward sinful human beings.

Today we live in a feel-good culture. We buy tapes that give us a boost to our low self-esteem. We want people to tell us things that make us feel good about ourselves, and we avoid those who might lead us to feel guilty about something. We believe material things will satisfy our inner hunger; temporarily, they might, but never for very long. Soon the hunger returns, and we seek more affirmation, the next acquisition or a new thrill, hoping to find satisfaction for the emptiness in our souls.

When I was a child, I always preferred to eat candy instead of meals (I still tend toward that weakness). It tasted so much better. Left to my own wisdom, I would have consumed candy for breakfast, lunch, and dinner. I ate so many sweets between meals that I was not usually hungry for regular food. Today we live in a candy-coated world where we want everything to taste good and go down easy. We don't like it when someone does something that interferes with what we think we need. God is supposed to make us feel good. When he doesn't, then we have no use for him.

God's loving-kindness is radically different from our understanding of love these days. Genuine love doesn't indulge or pacify. Real love helps; true love heals. It is because of his love for us that he tells us the truth about our condition and what we need to find life. Even if I don't like the bad news that I will get sick if I eat only candy every day, it is the truth. It is good for me to know the truth so that I can repent and change, lest I continue down the path of destruction. God warns us that disaster is ahead if we don't change our way of thinking and living. We often see God's judgment as a supreme act of unkindness. We view God as a mean-spirited Deity who wants to make us upset or afraid. But God's judgment pronounces loving truth. It accurately diagnoses our condition and shows us how to find healing. It is never kind to lie to someone, even if it does make them temporarily feel better.

Last year my mother was diagnosed with cancer. Though terrible news, we were relieved to finally get that diagnosis. For months her doctors had been telling her she just had bronchitis. She would get better, not to worry. The news that she only had bronchitis made her feel better in the short term, but her actual condition worsened. Only when she got an accurate diagnosis could she receive the appropriate treatment that could relieve her discomfort and improve the quality of her life.

We all have a sin problem that is like cancer. We may prefer not to know or to pretend it isn't fatal. We may tell ourselves that we're not as sick as someone else we know or that we're not too bad overall. Scripture warns us of our propensity to be self-deceived and to prefer lies to truth, especially in regard to our own selves. Jeremiah laments, "Prophets and priests alike, all practice deceit. They dress the wound of my people as though it were not serious. 'Peace, peace,' they say, when there is no peace" (Jeremiah 6:13-14).

God's loving-kindness not only accurately defines our problem but also provides the cure for our healing and well-being. "At one time we too were foolish, disobedient, deceived and enslaved by all kinds of passions and pleasures. We lived in malice and envy, being hated and hating one another. But when the kindness and love of God our Savior appeared, he saved us, not because of righteous things we had done, but because of his mercy" (Titus 3:3-5). The apostle Paul pleaded with people to be reconciled to God. He wrote, "God made him who had no sin to be sin for us, so that in him we might become the righteousness of God" (2 Corinthians 5:21). Jesus offers to take all the wrath and punishment that we deserve for our sin and rebellion upon himself so that we might be reconciled to God. What kind of love is that? Mysterious love, amazing grace. We do not deserve it. We cannot understand it. We can only receive it and be ever so grateful that, as a result, it changes us, and we want to become more like this God who loves us so. Oswald Chambers said, "The surest sign that God has done a work of grace in my heart is that I love Jesus Christ best, not weakly and faintly, not intellectually, but passionately, personally, and devotedly, overwhelming every other love of my life."[7]

The apostle Paul experienced the changed life of God's lovingkindness firsthand. Paul's given name was Saul. He was a Jewish scholar and a Pharisee whose goal was to stamp out Christians because he thought they were perverting the purity of Judaism with their crazy beliefs. One day as he was heading toward Damascus to take more Christian prisoners, a blinding light flashed down from heaven and knocked Saul to the ground. He heard a voice say to him, "Saul, Saul, why do you persecute me?" (Acts 9:4). Saul replied, "Who are you, Lord?" (verse 5). A blinding light and a voice from nowhere would scare and impress anyone, and Saul was surely frightened. But his response wasn't "Who are you?" but, "Who are you, *Lord?*" Saul recognized that the voice from above was none other than almighty God's.

The response was, "I am Jesus, whom you are persecuting" (verse 5). At that moment, Saul must have been terrified. He had been wrong—so very wrong. Jesus of Nazareth wasn't just a misguided zealot or a kook who claimed to be the Messiah. Jesus was Yahweh—Lord, God Almighty. What would he now do to Saul for persecuting him and throwing his followers in prison? Saul was in for a shocking surprise. Jesus didn't correct or scold him. He didn't threaten him with condemnation or wrath. Jesus loved Saul and lavished grace upon him by forgiving him. Jesus called Saul to be his ambassador—to serve him in furthering God's work.

God broke Saul's pride, and Saul's response was humility and deep repentance, which led to a totally changed life (Galatians 1:13-24). Andrew Murray said, "It's the sinner dwelling in the full light of God's holy, redeeming love, in the experience of that full indwelling of divine love that comes through Christ and the Holy Spirit, who cannot but be humble. Not being occupied with your sin, but being occupied with *God* brings deliverance from self."[8] Before he met Jesus, Saul was full of himself—his Jewish pedigree, his scholarly achievements, the rightness of his cause. Grace changed all that. Saul emptied himself of his self and became full of Christ.

Our Response

Seeing God clearly, in all his majesty, his greatness, and his mysterious loving-kindness toward undeserving humans ought to break our pride. Humility is a prerequisite to living in sync with our created purpose, which is to love God and enjoy him forever. Only when we see God clearly can we see ourselves clearly. He is holy; we are sinful. He is big; we are small. He is gracious; we are needy. He is not here to serve us; we are created to serve and glorify him. When we don't see him properly, our view of everything else, including ourselves, becomes skewed and distorted. "Great and marvelous are your deeds, Lord God Almighty. Just and true are your ways, King of the ages.

Who will not fear you, O Lord, and bring glory to your name? For you alone are holy. All nations will come and worship before you, for your righteous acts have been revealed" (Revelation 15:3-4).

To fear God in its fullest sense is to revere him and to be most deeply impressed with who he is.[9] In his book *The Fear of the Lord,* John Bevere explained, "The more extensive our comprehension of God's greatness…the greater our capacity for fear or reverence of Him."[10] To fear God is to be so enamored with the majesty, beauty, holiness, and grace of God that we long to know him. More than anything else we desire to be in an intimate and growing relationship with him. To fear God humbles us, because it places him, not us, at the center of life.

When we properly fear the Lord, we give God his rightful place in our lives by yielding our will to him. He is the author and the finisher of our faith. Who are we to question his ways? Andrew Murray said, "Humility is simply the disposition that prepares the soul for living on trust."[11] Scripture tells us that everything is for him, from him, and through him. He is the potter, and we are the clay. God's depth of knowledge and wisdom is beyond human comprehension, and we cannot fully know his ways. Therefore, since all these things are true, Paul exhorts us to yield ourselves fully to him as our reasonable form of worship (Romans 12:1). Honoring God through worship means more than singing songs during a Sunday morning church service. The Hebrew and Greek words here for *worship* mean "to bow down," "to prostrate oneself," and "to serve."

Worship does not make God worthy; he *is* worthy. But we declare it to be true by humbling ourselves as we acknowledge that truth with our heart, mind, and will. Worship means we consent to his lordship and yield ourselves to his transforming work in our lives. We can only do this honestly as we humble ourselves before him. "But be sure to fear the LORD and serve him faithfully with all your heart; consider what great things he has done for you" (1 Samuel 12:24).

PERSONAL APPLICATION

Are you most deeply impressed with the King of kings and Lord of lords? Or have other things grabbed your heart and stolen your affections? Take the time this week to worship, really worship, lowering yourself and yielding yourself, bowing internally and externally to the Lord, who is worthy of our praise, adoration, affection, attention, and energy.

Are You a Fan or a Friend?

As long as you are proud you cannot know God.

C. S. LEWIS

I have a picture in my office of me with Joni Eareckson Tada and her husband, Ken. Anyone looking at the photo would assume we are friends. I've read most of her books and support her ministry to the disabled. I know a lot about her and have admired her walk with God for years. But if we passed each other on the street, she wouldn't know me. We have no relationship. I'm a fan, not a friend. There is a huge difference.

I wonder sometimes if we don't confuse being a fan or admirer of Jesus with being his friend or having a personal relationship with him. We want what he has to offer us, like a happy life or a ticket to heaven, but that's about as far as it goes. Like one of my clients said, "I accepted Jesus when I was a kid. I have no doubt I'm going to heaven. Just because I don't read my Bible during the week or pray doesn't mean I don't believe in God. I do!"

I can't answer for this man's relationship with Jesus, but Christ himself cautioned those who thought they were his friends that the time would come when they might be surprised. When they roll out their spiritual pedigrees and acts of service on his behalf, he will say to them, "I never knew you" (Matthew 7:23).

Since our relationship with God is the source of lasting joy, let's turn our attention to what it means to have a friendship with God and a deepening intimacy with him.

Unconditional Love, Conditional Relationship

At times I think we equate the Bible's teaching on God's love to what it takes to have a relationship with Christ.

In the previous chapters we've seen that God passionately loves people. His love toward us is totally unconditional, meaning unmerited. Sometimes we mistakenly believe that we first need to prove ourselves or clean up our act before God will love us or want to be in relationship with us. We see our wrongs and weaknesses, and we feel so unworthy. Christ's love, however, is entirely undeserved and unearned. He sees our sins more clearly than even we see them, because he knows the deepest recesses of our hearts. Yet Jesus loves us so much that, even while we were in our most vile state, he willingly left his home in heaven to become like us and die for us so that we might have a relationship with him (Romans 5:8).

During one of my trips to the Philippines, my hosts took me to see what they call the "track people." These are squatters who live in makeshift houses slapped together with cardboard boxes and scrap metal, tottering inches from the railroad tracks. There is no plumbing, electricity, or glass windowpanes in these houses. Jagged windows cut in the cardboard walls provide an occasional wisp of steamy air. The community playground is the railroad tracks. Barefoot and nearly naked, the little ones play until a train blows its whistle, warning of its approach. The children quickly scramble off the tracks until the train passes. Extreme poverty, filth, and hopelessness add to the over-whelming difficulty of living day to day. While gaping at the whole wretched scene, God spoke to my heart. *Would you leave your nice, air-conditioned, four-bedroom home and come and live among these people to show them how much you love them? Would you be willing to spend thirty-three years with them, teaching them and caring for their needs, and then die for them? This is only a tiny glimpse of what I have done to show you I love you—and them.*

Gratitude welled up inside me. I felt grateful that Jesus loved me so much that he gladly left his beautiful heavenly palace to be born in a manger, as a squatter really, living in poverty so that I might have a relationship with God. But I also felt bad. I knew I would not have been willing to forsake my temporal comforts for these dear people. Perhaps for two weeks I could endure it, even enjoy some parts of it, but for years? Who would have that kind of selfless love? Jesus did.

God's love for us is undeserved and lavish, but it does not auto-matically guarantee that we will have a relationship with him. There is a barrier—something that separates us from God—and that barrier is sin. Our sin doesn't separate us from God's love (Romans 8:38-39), but it does separate us from his presence (Isaiah 59:1-2). Most often we think of sin as the bad things we do, like adultery or lying or steal-ing. That may be one reason why good people find it difficult to iden-tify themselves as sinners. They don't behave in blatantly sinful ways. They love their families, pay their taxes, and don't intentionally hurt other people. Yet God says their sin impedes a relationship with him.

In chapter 1 we looked at a young man who was interested in get-ting eternal life, but he really wasn't seeking a relationship with God. He wanted God's blessings, but on his own terms (see Mark 10:17-23). When Jesus told him to sell all his possessions, give them to the poor, and come and follow him, the man's face fell. These requirements were too steep; Jesus was asking for too much. Instead of following Christ, the rich young man walked away. In this story Jesus is not teaching us that a relationship with him requires us to sell everything we have and give it to the poor. Rather, he is saying that to have a relationship with God, we must enter it on his terms. Scripture says of this man, "Jesus looked at him and loved him" (verse 21), but then Jesus let him go his own way. Although Jesus loved the man, he was not willing to have a relationship with him on any other terms.

Perhaps a modern-day example might add to our understanding of the conditional relationship that Jesus offers us. Janice loved her husband, Stan. She longed for their relationship to be all God intended between a husband and wife. Stan readily received Janice's love, but he didn't want to put much work into building their marriage. In fact, Stan enjoyed living like a single man with the extra perks of married life. He came and went when he pleased, enjoyed flirting with other women, and refused to take responsibility for household chores and raising their children. He expected Janice to be attentive and available to him when he wanted her, yet he was consistently insensitive to her needs and acted selfishly most of the time. Eventually Janice discovered that Stan had been involved in several one-night sexual relationships with women at work. She finally began to understand that although she had a deep love for Stan, she could not and would not have an unconditional relationship with him. Janice knew she could not continue to act as if they were in a loving relationship when in reality they weren't.

It was time to have an honest talk. "Stan, I love you and want our marriage to work. However, I will not pretend that what we have together is a marriage. It is not. I feel like a prostitute and a maid. You are not willing to work on our relationship or keep yourself faithful to me. You act as if I don't matter, and my feelings are not important to you. You live for yourself, and everything is about you and what you want. I cannot and will not be in a relationship with you any longer on those terms."

Janice's words may appear drastic, but they convey the truth about her marriage to Stan. She didn't say these things to hurt Stan but to save their relationship. At times we may hear Jesus' words as harsh, even brutal, especially toward the religious leaders of his day. It is important to understand, though, that Jesus said these things so that those who thought they had a relationship with God would hear the truth and realize their complacency (or recognize their pride) and begin to change. He wanted to give them the opportunity to have an authentic relationship with him.

God calls people to a covenant relationship with him that is not unlike a marriage. He not only wants us to enjoy his love, he wants us to love him back (Deuteronomy 6:5). He not only promises us his faithfulness, he requires that we be faithful in return (Deuteronomy 4:23-24). The book of Hosea is a picture of God's love for his unfaithful spouse (Israel). He longs for her, but his relationship with her will remain broken until she is willing to change.

God is love. Because this is true, God can do no less than fully and completely love his creation. His love is always based on who he is; therefore, it is not dependent upon what we do or don't do. However, some things will hinder our relationship with him; other things make a relationship with God entirely impossible.

GOD OPPOSES THE PROUD

Our pride always gets in the way of our relationship with God. Sin, as God defines it, is much more extensive, insidious, and devious than a few outward behaviors. As we have already seen, sin is a pervasive attitude deep within our souls that seeks its own way, to be independent from God. "Pride is the attitude that exalts self above God."[1] That is our original sin. We are born self-centered, not God-centered. Like Adam and Eve, we want to be God. We refuse to acknowledge or submit to God's authority in our lives and his right to rule us. We want to be in charge or in control. We want to do things our way. We love being right and get defensive when people try to show us we are wrong. We want the credit and the glory for the good that is in us.

The sin of pride is not the same as the pride or good feeling that we experience when we have created something of beauty or worked hard at accomplishing a goal. The sinful pride that God opposes in its most blatant form is an internal orientation that refuses to acknowledge that we are dependent upon God's kindness and goodness for our very breath. The thought of needing God's grace or mercy or forgiveness is not only foreign, it is repulsive. The proud heart believes in himself, not in God.

In his classic book *Mere Christianity*, C. S. Lewis wrote, "According to Christian teachers, the essential vice, the utmost evil, is Pride. Unchastity, anger, greed, drunkenness, and all that, are mere fleabites in comparison: it was through Pride that the devil became the devil: Pride leads to every other vice: it is the complete anti-God state of mind."[2]

Let's look at a sample of what the Bible says about pride and a relationship with God.

The arrogant cannot stand in your presence. (Psalm 5:5)

In his pride the wicked does not seek him;
   in all his thoughts there is no room for God. (Psalm 10:4)

Though the LORD is on high, he looks upon the lowly,
 but the proud he knows from afar. (Psalm 138:6)

The LORD detests all the proud of heart.
 Be sure of this: They will not go unpunished.
                                                    (Proverbs 16:5)

"The pride of your heart has deceived you,
 you who live in the clefts of the rocks
 and make your home on the heights,
you who say to yourself,
 'Who can bring me down to the ground?'
Though you soar like the eagle
 and make your nest among the stars,
 from there I will bring you down,"
                                    declares the LORD. (Obadiah 3-4)

God opposes the proud
 but gives grace to the humble. (James 4:6)

If angels were expelled from God's presence because of pride, we cannot expect God to be friends with us when we are full of self-importance. Pride deceives us into thinking that we have no need of God. God loves us and seeks a personal relationship with people, but when we deny we need what he offers us, a relationship with him is impossible.

Most of us would not be so foolish and bold as to tell God we don't need him outright. Our pride works in much more subtle ways. Of course we need him. We need him to help us succeed at what we set out to do, to make us happy and give us a wonderful life. But then, as Mark Buchanan wrote, "Jesus only exists to propel me toward personal fulfillment, when I've got time and inclination. *That* Jesus I accept on my terms."[3]

The God of Our Own Making

One of the questions I ask when people come to see me for counseling is, "Are you interested in a deeper relationship with God?" I am always curious as to their response. Those who say no perplex me. Why wouldn't anyone feel a need for a closer relationship with God? Perhaps he has been disillusioned or hurt. Maybe she's angry or misinformed. Jill was someone who said "no way" when I first broached that question.

"I'm done with God," she scoffed. "I don't want anything to do with him."

"What happened?" I inquired, curious as to what could have possibly caused her to feel so angry.

"My roommate at college told me that God loved me and wanted a personal relationship with me. She told me all I needed to do was ask Jesus into my heart, and he would come in. I did that, but nothing happened. I waited and I prayed, but I never felt his love. For a while I went to church and read the Bible, but I'm tired of waiting. Why should I believe in him? He never did anything for me!"

"What about the cross and forgiveness?" I gently offered. Jesus showed how much he loved you by dying for you."

"Oh that," she said. "The cross was a long time ago. I don't need forgiveness. I need to be loved, and I don't feel anything from God. I thought God was supposed to make me happy."

Perhaps the reason that Jill found her relationship with "God" so empty was because the God of the Bible wasn't in the relationship. Jill sought a Jesus she could control, one who would do her bidding, not a Jesus worthy of her worship and repentance. Larry Crabb wrote, "When helping people to feel loved and worthwhile has become the central mission of the church, God is used more than worshiped— and that doesn't work."[4] Like the rich young ruler, Jill wanted the blessings of a relationship with God but on her terms. No wonder she became disappointed. God doesn't relate to us on our terms. If he did, we'd have to wonder, *Who is really God?*

Clients who indicate that they desire a better relationship with God also arouse my curiosity. I wonder what they hope to gain from a deepening friendship with God. Like Jill, many of us are looking for more blessings, more benefits from God, instead of knowing God himself. For a long time, my relationship with God was superficial. God was gracious in my ignorance and immaturity. As I look back, I see that my prayers were usually one-way conversations. I told God what I wanted him to do for me, but I didn't listen carefully to what he wanted from me. *God, could you help me be more successful or more popular? Lord, please get me out of this mess. Dear Jesus, bless my business or my ministry.*

The deceptive part of this kind of relationship with God is that often there is absolutely nothing wrong or sinful in what we want God to do for us. It is not as if we are asking God to bless our plans to rob a bank or to help us kill our neighbor. We want him to give us a good feeling about ourselves or to assist us so that we get the job we want or into the college we've applied to. We want him to get us to the airport on time so we won't miss our flight to Disney World or to give us a husband or wife who is more spiritual or sexual or thoughtful or responsible.

But our desires are still all about us—what we want, what we long for, our goals for our lives, what we think we need the most. Like Eli's sons, we are religious *and* self-centered (1 Samuel 2:22-24). We have reduced God to our helper, made in our image, bowing to our agenda. A god to help us when we're stuck and to support us in our weak moments. He becomes a crutch; prayer, a prop. Whether subtly or boldly, we don't abandon ourselves to God for his purposes, but we want him to bless our purposes. We want to experience his love and his goodness or have his power or favor when we're in a jam, but we will decide when and how. We have created a god to meet our expectations and fulfill our desires.

Fénelon wrote: "Alas, how many souls there are, their own masters, who want to do good and to love God, but according to their own pleasure and on their own initiative; who would like to make rules for God, as to how he is to satisfy them and to attract them to him! They want to serve him and to possess him, but they do not want to give themselves to him and to allow themselves to be possessed."[5] *This* Jesus is not the Lord of our lives; he is the servant of our desires, making a deepening friendship with God impossible.

What Is Necessary to Have a Friendship with God?

Up to now we have examined our natural innate tendency to rebel against God and his ways. We've looked at our pride problem and our proclivity to believe our ways are better than God's and that we know better than he does how to make our lives work. We have seen our inherent selfishness and self-centeredness even as believers when we try to use God to service our own agenda. But if we want a genuine and deep friendship with Jesus, the God of the Bible, we must change that way of thinking and relating. This conversion process begins as we realize that our way of being, thinking, and relating has been wrong and severely limited and that God's way is true, good, and right.

A Friendship with God Begins with Repentance

Jesus called this process of changing our mind, of turning away from our sin and our self-centeredness, repentance. He said that repentance is absolutely necessary in order to have a relationship with him. (See Matthew 4:17; Mark 1:15; Luke 13:5.)

Today we don't often hear that we must repent. The word itself scares us. We imagine a wild-eyed, bushy-haired zealot carrying a big sign with John 3:16 scrawled across it in bold black letters, pacing and yelling, "Repent or you're going to hell!" Yet repentance is so crucial to our relationship with God, we cannot be his friends without it.

Repentance comes from the Greek word *metanoia* and "involves both a turning from sin and a turning to God."[6] When Jesus calls humankind to repent, he doesn't merely call us to a casual change of opinion but a revolutionary conversion of our perspective. He doesn't teach us only to regret our sin but to totally reorient our direction and purpose for life. Repentance changes us. We no longer live for the same things that we lived for before. We now see those things differently. We see them as empty, decaying, and destructive to our welfare. Repentance involves turning from darkness to light, from self-orientation to God-orientation.

Repentance is not a once-and-done event but an ongoing process. Conversion continues day by day as we learn to take all our thoughts captive to the obedience of Christ and to allow God to transform our mind (Romans 12:2). Repentance doesn't occur only in our heart but also in our habits. As we learn to listen to God and trust him, he shows us more and more true reality and what needs to be transformed so that we may reflect his image clearly through our lives. The fruit of repentance is a changed heart, whereby our deepest desire is no longer to please ourselves but to please God.

Humility Is Foundational to Repentance

When we see our own wrongs and acknowledge them before God and others, we've taken an important first step. But there is more if we are to fully understand repentance. Earlier in chapter 4 we saw that Judas was "seized with remorse" (Matthew 27:3) after he betrayed Christ. Judas acknowledged his sin, yet instead of turning to God, he held on to his pride and destroyed himself. He would not humble himself to depend upon Christ for forgiveness. Judas sought a solution that would permit him to save face: suicide.

Anthony was arrested for soliciting a prostitute. He knew that any day his name would appear in the newspaper and he'd be exposed. Anthony felt tremendous guilt. Fear and shame overwhelmed him. He knew what he did was wrong and wrote a long confession to his wife before he shot himself in their garage. Instead of repentance, Anthony experienced merely regret and disgust with himself. He was humiliated, but sadly, Anthony did not humble himself to receive what he most desperately needed—forgiveness from God and from his wife.

It is hard to face the truth that we need God. It wounds our self-sufficiency and our pride. We prefer to live as if we can fix our own problems, make our own decisions, pay our own way. As we learned in chapter 2, humility begins when we recognize our poverty in spirit, our neediness. Humility is born when we confess it. The blind beggar knew his neediness. Others tried to quiet him, but he was desperate. He shouted, "Jesus, Son of David, have mercy on me!" (Luke 18:38).

Like the blind beggar, at times we realize our neediness. Several years ago my good friend Georgia needed a bone-marrow transplant to fight the breast cancer that threatened her life. She could not do it on her own. Not only did she need others' help with her daily care and household tasks, she also required assistance in meeting the needs of her ten-year-old son. And she humbly and gratefully received what she could not do for herself.

Most of the time we aren't as mindful of our neediness. We think we're doing just fine. We feel strong or secure, confident and self-sufficient. Don't let those feelings mislead you. Jesus' words confront our stubborn independence: "You say, 'I am rich; I have acquired wealth and do not need a thing.' But you do not realize that you are wretched, pitiful, poor, blind and naked." Jesus also said, "Those whom I love I rebuke and discipline. So be earnest, and repent" (Revelation 3:17,19). One of the saddest portions of Scripture illustrates our tendency to sacrifice our relationship with God and our well-being because of our pride. "Obey me, and I will be your God and you will be my people. Walk in all the ways I command you, that it may go well with you. But they did not listen or pay attention; instead, they followed the stubborn inclinations of their evil hearts. They went backward and not forward" (Jeremiah 7:23-24).

We will always forsake a genuine walk with God if we think that we know better than he does what we need for life. One of our biggest obstacles to intimacy with God is when we see that we need God for forgiveness but fail to grasp that we need him for *everything* that makes life good. We invite God along as our helper but don't want to surrender to him as Lord.

WHY DO YOU CALL ME "LORD"?

Jesus repeatedly asked his followers, "Who do you say that I am?" For a while they weren't sure. When Jesus stilled the turbulent sea, the disciples were terrified and whispered among themselves, "Who is this man?" When he performed healing miracles, they were amazed. They enjoyed his company and were impressed with his power, but they still weren't quite sure who Jesus really was. Finally Jesus asked Peter directly, "But what about you? Who do you say that I am?" (Matthew 16:15).

Each of us is asked this same question. "But what about you? Who do you say that I am?" Is Jesus a rescuer we call upon only when we need help? Is he someone we praise when things are good and accuse when things are bad? Perhaps some of us see Jesus as our errand boy or cosmic Santa Claus. Or maybe he is our buddy, our man upstairs, or our higher power. Our answer to Jesus' question, "Who do you say that I am?" will determine whether we become his friends or remain fans. Perhaps it would be helpful for you to stop here for a moment and answer this question for yourself. Peter answered Jesus' question correctly when he said, "You are the Christ, the Son of the living God" (Matthew 16:16).

Jesus asked his followers a second question, one perhaps even more important than the first. This question is one we must stop and answer too if we want a deepening friendship with God. Jesus did not want pretenders or fans to deceive themselves into believing that they were his friends. He challenged their complacency and questioned their relationship with him when he probed, "Why do you call me, 'Lord, Lord,' and do not do what I say?" (Luke 6:46). Jesus warned his fans not to fool themselves by calling him Lord when they lived their lives for their own selfish purposes.

Some of us who want Jesus to be our Savior can admit our need for forgiveness but fail to worship him as Lord—the supreme authority in our lives. We are sure we can't get to heaven without him, but somehow we're not quite convinced that *we* still are not the best ones to run our own lives. We are reluctant to surrender ourselves to him and permit him to be Lord over everything. We do not love Jesus first or honor him fully in our lives. We are more impressed by the things of this world than the things of God. John Bevere observed, "The accurate measurement of our true spiritual condition lies in our actual obedience to His will."[7]

God loves the humble heart, and to deepen our friendship with him, we must humble ourselves before him. But how do we grow to develop a heart of genuine selflessness?

PERSONAL APPLICATION

It is time to evaluate your relationship with God. Are you a friend or a fan? Do you call him Lord but refuse to do what he says? Do you live as if he is your servant, or are you willingly his?

A genuine relationship with God begins by being honest with ourselves and with God. We only see ourselves truthfully through his lens, the Bible. We must admit to ourselves and to him that we desperately need him: for forgiveness and for everything that makes life good. Andrew Murray wrote, "Humility is simply the sense of entire nothingness that comes when we see how truly God is all, and in which we make way for God to be all!"[8]

Write in your journal a prayer to God, asking him to help you see with a new set of eyes. Begin repenting of your pride and stubborn inclination to go your own way. Ask him to change your prideful heart to a heart of humility.

8

Growing in Selflessness

For you can have no greater sign of a more confirmed pride,
than when you think that you are humble enough.

WILLIAM LAW

L ast year I gave up cardiovascular exercise. It's not that I don't
work out; I do. But I reasoned that if I only had a limited
amount of time to exercise, I would be better off lifting weights so I
could see some visible results—muscles. What I didn't know was
waste products that accumulate in the muscles through weight training only get flushed out by freshly oxygenated blood. So this year I
resumed my aerobics in addition to my strength-training exercises.

Often my spiritual growth takes a similar path. I concentrate
my efforts on what shows—like loving others or disciplining my
tongue—and tend to forsake the inner work that makes those efforts
more productive. I neglect to develop and strengthen the virtue of
the heart that is foundational for the rest of the fruit of the Spirit to
flourish.

As with our physical bodies, humility functions as the heart and
lungs of a person's spiritual growth. By itself, humility is invisible
and quiet, but without it, genuine spiritual maturity is impossible.

Humility strengthens and energizes all the other virtues, flushing out pride and selfishness when they start to accumulate. Andrew Murray wrote, "The *lack* of humility is the sufficient explanation of every defect and failure."[1] Trying to be a spiritual person without humility is like trying to do sustained weight training with a weak heart and lungs. It is impossible.

When we see someone who is healthy and in good shape, we don't notice his or her heart and lungs. Rather, we're impressed with the outward manifestations of strength—bulging biceps or ripped abdominal muscles—and want to learn the easiest and fastest way to achieve the same results. Millions of dollars are spent every year advertising pills and devices that promise to get our bodies into great shape without any effort. Likewise, we have often looked for the biblical shortcut instead of doing the work required to develop the inner posture that supports a deeper intimacy with God and others. We may want to look spiritually strong and have great relationships, but we also want it to be easy and fast.

Real maturity takes time. We must make the necessary effort to cultivate a humble heart. Gary Thomas wrote, "Humility is at root a celebration of our freedom in Christ; we are freed from having to make a certain impression or create a false front. Humility places within us a desire for people to know us as we are, not as we hope to be and not as we think they want us to be or even as we think we should be. Real growth cannot begin until we come to this point."[2]

MAKE THE EFFORT

Once I grasped just how important cardiovascular exercise is to my overall well-being, I had a lot of work to do. Just a year earlier I had trained myself to run two miles. When I tried to run again this year, I found myself back at my beginning levels. I couldn't believe how much ground I had lost. Although I had developed other muscles, my year of neglect had weakened my heart and lungs.

Some people resist doing the work required to mature as a Christian. They think that to exercise and practice spiritual disciplines is characteristic of a works-righteousness approach to God—one that attempts to earn our salvation. Not so. There is nothing we can do to earn God's forgiveness or his favor. However, God's Word also tells us that as disciples of Christ we should train ourselves to be godly (1 Timothy 4:7). Peter says we should "make every effort" with regard to cultivating our spiritual character (2 Peter 1:5-8). And Jesus says that if we hear what he says but don't put it into practice, we are fools (Luke 6:46-49).

Salvation is God's work. However, our sanctification (spiritual growth and maturity) is a combined effort. Some is up to us; some is God's doing. Elijah hauled the stones and poured the water; God produced the fire. (For the story, read 1 Kings 18:16-39.) Jesus sanctified himself and prayed that we, too, would be sanctified (John 17:17). *Vine's Expository Dictionary* says sanctification "is not vicarious, i.e., it cannot be transferred or imputed, it is an individual possession, built up, little by little, as the result of obedience to the Word of God, and of following the example of Christ...in the power of the Holy Spirit."[3] We are to make every effort—till Christ be fully formed in us (Galatians 4:19).

EXERCISING HUMILITY

As we look now at some ways we can develop and grow in humility, we also need to realize that this virtue is something we work toward, though we will never fully attain it this side of heaven. Gary Thomas notes, "We don't become humble as much as we learn to practice humility. The virtues aren't a state of being as much as they are inner disciplines after which we aspire. We enter into the virtues by degrees, and perhaps nowhere is this as true as it is with the virtue of humility."[4] William Law further advises, "Now in order to begin, and set out well, in the practice of humility, you must take it for granted that you are proud, that you have all your life been more or less infected with this unreasonable temper."[5] Our pride is so slippery and deceptive. No matter how faithfully we learn to practice selflessness, watch out! The moment we believe we've become humble enough, we're not humble. We fall right back into pride, admiring ourselves because we're becoming so humble.

As we take a look at some exercises we can practice to cultivate humility, please understand that what we learn at one level, we may not find as easy to implement on another. As I watched my daughter, Amanda, take piano lessons for more than thirteen years, I grew in my knowledge of notes, timing, and piano playing. Of course, I never actually learned to play the piano since I failed to put any of my *head knowledge* into daily practice. Many of us do this in our spiritual lives as well. We absorb good teaching; we just never apply it. Then we wonder why we don't manifest much spiritual fruit or maturity in our day-to-day lives.

Godly character is formed in us as we consistently exercise and practice these virtues within the daily responsibilities of life. Law advises, "Every person, when he first applies himself to the exercise of this virtue of humility, must…consider himself as a learner, that is to learn something that is contrary to former tempers and habits of mind, and which can only be got by daily and constant practice."[6]

There are at least three essential attitudes of the heart that we must regularly nourish and exercise for humility to grow in us. Christ demonstrated these perfectly throughout his life, and because we aim to be like him, we should also aim to nurture these habits in our own heart and life. First, it is crucial that we be committed to honesty with ourselves, with others, and with God. This keeps us from being blinded by our own pride and reminds us of our smallness. (Although Christ had no pride, he was honest with God, himself, and others.) Second, we must daily yield to God as Lord in our lives, trusting him as the One who knows best what we need in all things. Third, it's vital that we cultivate a genuine desire to selflessly serve others.

Two words of caution. It is tempting when talking about selfishness and pride to think of everyone else we know who has those sins and try to get them to develop these disciplines. The following suggested practices are for *you* to grow in humility, not for you to get someone else to grow in humility. Remember, selflessness is to be desired, but it must be personally decided, not coerced. Therefore, only the one seeking it can practice these disciplines. Second, we must understand that the inner posture of selflessness takes a lifetime to mature. Try not to feel overwhelmed. It may only take you fifteen minutes to read this chapter but years to put it into practice. Begin where you are today, and daily ask God to help your inner life as well as your outer life become permeated with the meekness of Jesus.

1. Exercising Courageous Commitment to Truth

Humility is possible only when we leave the darkness of our human reasoning and start to walk in the light of God. Not too long ago I bought one of those lighted magnifying mirrors. Both my husband and I were horrified at what we saw when we peered into the bigger-than-life truth teller. We found hairs where we shouldn't have hairs and no hair where there once was hair. The makeup that I thought I had carefully applied was uneven, and I saw lots of tiny new wrinkles starting to emerge. "Oh my!" I moaned. "I'm a mess."

Isaiah, a righteous man, felt the same way when he encountered God. He saw himself in a much clearer light and cried out something similar about himself (Isaiah 6:1-5). Like Isaiah, we only see ourselves accurately when we are next to the big light. Fénelon taught:

> As the inner light increases, you will see the imperfections which you have seen heretofore as basically much greater and more harmful than you had seen them up to the present.... But this experience, far from discouraging you, will help to uproot all your self-confidence, and to raze to the ground the whole edifice of pride. Nothing marks so much the solid advancement of a soul, as this view of his wretchedness without anxiety and without discouragement.[7]

The following exercises will help you practice walking in the truth. They will help you learn to be more honest with yourself, with others, and with God. Remember, being committed to something in theory is one thing; actually having the courage to live out that commitment is another. The function of these exercises is to confront our pride and unbelief and to break up the stony ground of stubbornness and self-deceit that pervades our heart and our relationships.

Exercise One: Practice Self-Awareness and Self-Examination

Many of us give little or no thought to who we are, why we are here, or what we are doing or thinking or feeling. Sometimes we are so busy we don't leave space in our schedules for reflection and review. For some, this is purposeful; we'd rather not look. We prefer to remain in the dark about our true condition. For others, we simply aren't intentional enough to regularly take stock.

Without self-awareness, we will not have the capacity for truth because we will not be able to evaluate ourselves under the light of God's Word. The psalmist prayed, "Search me, O God, and know my heart; test me and know my anxious thoughts. See if there is any offensive way in me, and lead me in the way everlasting" (Psalm 139:23-24). When we leave no time for reflection or quiet meditation, we don't give God the opportunity to show us our heart.

Because of our tremendous capacity to be deceived and to self-deceive, the only truth we can count on is God's truth. Theresa of Avila said: "We shall never succeed in knowing ourselves unless we seek to know God: let us think of His greatness and then come back to our own baseness; by looking at His purity we shall see our foulness; by meditating upon His humility, we shall see how far we are from being humble.... Anything white looks very much whiter against something black, just as the black looks blacker against the white."[8] And John Calvin wrote: "No man can survey himself without forthwith turning his thoughts towards God, in whom he lives and moves. Man never attains to a true self-knowledge until he has previously contemplated the face of God and come down after such contemplation to look into himself."[9]

Some areas that we need to put under the light of God's truth include the quality of our relationship with him, the stewardship we are exercising over our lives, and our interactions with others. The following questions will help you examine yourself in these areas. Answer them thoughtfully, perhaps by journalizing your answers as prayers to

God. Although it is good not to rush, try to get through all of the questions in a short period of time. Otherwise you may not see overall life patterns, which are important. Perhaps a day's retreat or several closely spaced periods of focused attention will help you gain the perspective God wants you to have about yourself.

One word of caution: As we learned in chapter 4, there are those who have been morbidly introspective and self-conscious their entire lives. They are fearful, anxious, and insecure because they not only overexamine themselves but do so with a microscope. The problem with these folks is that their measuring rod is their own idealized version of their perfect self, not God's Word. Oswald Chambers cautioned us when he said: "I am called to live in perfect relation to God so that my life produces a longing after God in other lives, not admiration for myself. Thoughts about myself hinder my usefulness to God. God is not after perfecting me to be a specimen in His showroom; He is getting me to the place where He can use me."[10]

If you tend to fall into morbid analysis, guard yourself against letting your reflections lead you into old patterns of shame and self-hatred, which have more to do with being disappointed in yourself than they do with growing in humility.

Questions to Evaluate Your Relationship with God

Is God first in my life? How have I grown in my love relationship with Jesus? Do I love him with all my heart, soul, mind, and strength? What other loves keep me from loving God first? Am I most deeply impressed with him, or do other things grab my heart and attention? What are those things? Do I treat his Word lightly or casually? Do I obey him? Am I talking with him regularly? Do I listen to what he tells me? Is he the Lord of my life or the servant of my desires?

Questions to Evaluate Your Stewardship of Your Life

How do I see myself? Am I aware of my daily need for God's forgiveness and grace? Do I care for myself in the way God instructs (see chapter 9), or am I self-indulgent or morbidly preoccupied with myself, my flaws, and my imperfections? Do I believe what God tells me about who I am? Do I thank him for the gifts and talents he has given me to glorify him and serve others? Am I using my gifts and abilities for his purposes or for my own? Do I readily correct myself when I am wrong, sinful, or thinking untrue thoughts, or do I ignore them, excuse myself, or slide into self-hatred or self-pity?

Questions to Evaluate Your Interactions with Others

Do I extend myself and concern myself with the needs of others, or am I more focused on my own interests? How do I treat people? Am I prejudiced, intolerant, or condescending toward any particular group? Minorities? Women? A specific ethnic or religious group? Am I kind, generous, self-controlled, meek, forbearing, loving, submissive, patient, and gentle? Would others evaluate me this way? Do I consider another person's ideas, needs, and feelings as important as my own? How would my spouse describe me? My children? People at work, school, or church? Do I put on one face in public and another in private? Am I teachable, or do I always have to be right?

Exercise Two: Practice Confession

Confession is another exercise by which you can cultivate honesty with yourself, God, and others as you acknowledge truth by speaking it aloud. Often we think of confession in terms of admitting our sin before God. Although this is essential, it is not the only aspect of confession. Jesus had no sin to confess, yet he regularly acknowledged to others his purpose, his position, and his dependence upon the Father (see, for example, John 8:28,54; 14:10).

Many of the psalms are confessional psalms from the heart of a penitent sinner. Many others are prayers of truth that acknowledge the reality of our smallness and God's greatness.

The apostle Paul also instructed us to confess with our mouth our relationship with Christ (Romans 10:9-10), and he said that one day all will confess that Jesus is Lord (Romans 14:11). How many times have I kept my lips locked from sharing about Christ with others because I worried what others might think of me? My pride and/or my fear of people sometimes keeps me from humbling myself. When we are humble, however, we are not ashamed to confess the truth; we are not afraid to say that God is God. He alone is worthy of our love, honor, and praise.

A regular practice of public confession of the worthiness of God (called praise and worship) draws our self-oriented heart up and out of ourselves and places it squarely on the loveliness of Christ and the goodness, holiness, and majesty of God. Praise and worship move us away from being self-centered people and toward being God-centered people. Calvin Miller put it this way: "We bow to him, leaving self and self-interest behind us. At that moment, it is no longer enough to explain ourselves by owning up to our own names. We must own up to his. We must confess him before others...and unashamedly say that our own identity is of such small importance we have replaced it with his."[11]

As we practice confession before God, we come to own our sin as our sin—no excuses, no blaming others. It is also helpful in nurturing humility to confess our sin to one another (James 5:16). Gary Thomas warns, "Secrets are spiritual cancers. They allow a sinful action to become a habit until hell has a feast on what started out as 'one little sin.' Confession keeps us uncomfortable in our sin and forces us to seek a resolution."[12]

Last, in this process of self-examination, the Holy Spirit reveals our failures and sins against one another. A commitment to truth requires that we learn to confess our sins to those we have sinned against and to ask their forgiveness. Genuine confession, born out of a contrite heart, cultivates humility. Sincere confession is difficult and requires courage. It wounds our ego to admit our faults to one another. Our pride would rather stay deceived or ignorant about who we really are or what we have really done. It's easier to blame others than to seek their forgiveness.

Humility exercised through honest confession leads to deeper intimacy with God and others. Sadly, many of us would rather not lower ourselves. Instead, we further damage our relationship with God and others by erecting walls of stubborn silence, pride, and shame. Recently one of my clients shared with me how she caught her husband in a serious sexual sin. Rather than engage in honest self-examination and commit to seeking truth, he shifted blame. "You're making too much of this," he chided. Instead of confessing his sin, he made excuses and back-pedaled: "Everybody does it. There is nothing wrong with it." Instead of healing and restoring their relationship, his pride led to brokenness and separation. Humble confession of sin not only cleanses our souls, it can bring healing to wounded relationships.

Exercise Three: Practice Accepting Criticism

There are many exercises that would give you practice in walking in truth, but the last one I'll encourage you to learn is to gratefully accept criticism from others. Ouch! Who likes that? Yet humility opens up a new way of seeing, living, and relating to others. It teaches us to think of God's agenda and not our own. Humility calls us to perceive the criticisms of others as "good for us" because they teach us not to think more highly of ourselves than we ought (Romans 12:3).

A person who desires to be humble and is committed to internal and relational honesty realizes that all criticism contains at least a grain of truth. Next time someone makes a disparaging remark, instead of becoming defensive or argumentative, receive it graciously, knowing that it is for your good that God allowed this person to correct you. Perhaps most of it isn't true, but look for what is true. Thank the person who has brought the problem or character flaw or sin to your attention, and prayerfully bring it before the Lord. He will help you sort out the truth from the falsehood. "Let the righteous strike me; it shall be a kindness. And let him reprove me; it shall be as excellent oil; let my head not refuse it" (Psalm 141:5, NKJV).

2. Daily Yielding to God as Lord in Everything

Many of us (myself included) struggle to fully yield ourselves to God in everything. Although our head knows we should, our pride resents and resists giving up the reins of our life. Surrender is birthed in a humble heart. We surrender not because we're defeated, but because we believe God knows better what we need—even if it's hard. We believe that real joy comes only when we are united with God; therefore, his will becomes our will, and nothing we desire can compete with our ultimate desire to be one with him.

Part of nurturing humility through yielding to Christ's lordship means that we grow to think differently about ourselves, about life, and about our purpose. Paul wrote that we're to have the same attitude, or mind (NKJV), that Christ had (Philippians 2:5). Part of our spiritual growth involves "renewing" our mind (Romans 12:2). This does not merely mean that we learn to have good thoughts instead of bad thoughts, or pure thoughts instead of evil thoughts. Rather, our thoughts are changed from self-oriented thoughts to God-oriented thoughts, from self-focused, self-centered thoughts to God-centered, God-honoring thoughts. Our inner motivation begins to shift from "me first" to "God first." Our primary question shifts from "What's in it for me?" to "What do you want me to do, Lord?"

Exercise One: Practice Accepting Hardship

One of the things we can practice in our desire to yield more fully to the Lord in all areas of our lives is to accept the hardship he allows in our lives as being for our good. Accepting hardship does not mean that we do not feel the pain involved. It means that we receive the difficulties the Lord allows in our lives without resentment. We bow to God's sovereignty and trust in his wisdom.

I seem to do this more readily in the bigger trials of life. *Okay, I'll trust you Lord with this.* (Perhaps it's easier because in these moments I feel small and powerless, and so it is easier to admit that I am). Yet in my day-to-day hardships—losing my keys, sitting in endless traffic jams, dealing with rude clerks or long lines—I find it much harder to let go of my agenda and humbly accept my circumstances, yielding to God's plan for my day. Instead of "I'll trust you in this, Lord," what pours out of my mouth is, "Why, Lord? This isn't fair!" Or, "I don't deserve this!" As I was writing this section, I developed a case of poison ivy. I laughed as I caught myself thinking, *Not now, I have so much to do!* But God gently reminded me, *Here is your opportunity to practice what you're writing. Accept this small hardship with trust instead of impatience or irritation!* Joy comes when we say, "Yes, Lord."

The next time you face a small hardship or inconvenience (tomorrow probably), instead of fighting against it or merely resigning yourself to get through it, choose to humbly consent to God's work in your life. Ask him, "What do you want me to see in this moment? To learn? To practice?" "The person who lives in right relationship with God does it by embracing what God arranges for him. Doing things for God is the opposite of entering into what God does for you" (Galatians 3:11, MSG).

The psalmist declared, "You are good, and what you do is good" (Psalm 119:68). Jesus learned obedience in the things he suffered (Hebrews 5:8), and so will we, as we yield our will to God's plan. Fénelon said, "When we give ourselves entirely to the designs of God for us, we are as willing to be deprived of consolations as to enjoy them. Often a deprivation that disturbs and humbles us is more useful to us than an abundance of comforting."[13] In his book *Seeking the Face of God,* Gary Thomas wrote, "The biggest block to our surrender is not our appetites and wayward desires, but our addiction to running our own lives. Surrender would be easy if it allowed us to merely sacrifice a few leaves, a few choice sins. But God wants more. God's ax hits the trunk."[14]

As we've come to learn, we don't always understand God. He is bigger, smarter, and much more powerful than we are. Although in the midst of hardship we'd like to understand what God's up to, the surrendered heart acknowledges that he doesn't owe us an explanation, and in humility we would never demand one. Habakkuk, one of the prophets of the Old Testament, struggled to understand God. In the end he willingly surrendered: He proclaimed:

> Though the fig tree does not bud
> and there are no grapes on the vines,
> though the olive crop fails
> and the fields produce no food,

though there are no sheep in the pen
and no cattle in the stalls,
yet I will rejoice in the LORD,
I will be joyful in God my Savior. (Habakkuk 3:17-18)

Loving and trusting God, especially when we don't understand, deeply pleases and satisfies him. It is like pouring sweet scented oil on his feet—it ministers to him and makes him glad.

Exercise Two: Practice Submitting to Others

All believers are to practice the discipline of honoring and willingly submitting to one another (Ephesians 5:21). Humility makes submission toward others possible. We learn to willingly yield our way to others' preferences and desires. We want to serve them, honor them, and meet their needs, even if it means we must sacrifice ourselves.

One of the first questions I get whenever I talk about submission, whether from wives or the general Christian population, is "Does submission mean I have to be a doormat?" The answer is no and yes. Humble submission is a voluntary position we take. Biblical submission is never coerced. When Jesus told us to go the extra mile or turn the other cheek, I believe the message he was emphasizing was that even when someone forces you to do one thing, you can willingly and humbly do more (see Matthew 5:38-42). Lauren White wisely noted, "It's not that the humble let others trample over them, but that they recognize and subject themselves to higher purposes."[15]

One of the essential components of humility is self-forgetfulness. This is not natural to our humanity. The virtue of humility teaches us not to worry about ourselves so much, whether we are being regarded or treated well, whether our rights are being violated or we are being taken advantage of. Laying down our rights by voluntarily submitting to others, however, is not something we do randomly, recklessly permitting others to sin against us. That would be foolish. Rather, we intentionally yield ourselves to another for a purpose that must not be destructive or sinful.

The apostle Paul gives us some good reasons to lay down our rights. He tells us that he laid down his rights so that the gospel would not be hindered (1 Corinthians 9:12). He also encourages believers to submit to one another out of reverence for Christ (Ephesians 5:21), for the unity of the body (Ephesians 4:2-3), and for the good of the other person (1 Corinthians 10:24). Submission ascribes honor and preference to others above ourselves.

Humility teaches us that the law of love *always* supersedes our rights. Paul speaks about our right to eat certain foods or to enjoy practices that we do not find sinful. Yet, he cautions, if our action hurts another, the law of love is higher than our right to please or enjoy ourselves (1 Corinthians 10:23–11:1). Humility and the practice of submission put the love for Christ and the love for others and their welfare above pleasing our own selves.

3. Nurturing a Servant's Heart

Richard Foster wrote, "More than any other single way, the grace of humility is worked into our lives through the Discipline of service."[16] We can deepen our internal humility by choosing servanthood.

The Old Testament offers us a picture of voluntary slavery. After six years of service, a slave was to be freed. However, if the slave declared his love for his family and his master and wanted to stay, the master would take him before the judges and have his ear pierced, and he would become a slave for life (Exodus 21:2-6). This lifelong commitment is the picture we are to have of service. Servanthood is an inner attitude we have about ourselves, not merely acts of service that we occasionally do for others. With the latter we have a tendency to puff ourselves up. *Boy aren't I doing something nice for those people?* Oswald Chambers warns us to "beware of anything that puts you in the superior person's place."[17] Although servanthood is a great way to get out of the superior person's place, acts of service might put you right back in there. When we have a servant's heart, we are available to God to serve him and serve others—whatever he asks us to do, whomever he asks us to serve. We are not in charge; he is. We serve God and others because we have declared our love for him, and what he desires is the most important thing to us.

Exercise One: Practice Volunteering for Menial Tasks

Humble service is the act of dying to self in the mundane, daily chores and trivial things of life. Christ served others in many ways. He healed the sick, fed the multitudes, taught the disciples and the religious leaders. Those tasks seem much more glamorous and important than the ordinary and somewhat degrading job of foot washing. Yet it was this daily task that Jesus used to teach us about service. We are to take the low place, to volunteer for jobs that no one wants. We resist taking the menial jobs when we haven't lowered ourselves on the inside. We don't want to be last; we'd rather be first. We want to do great things, be noticed and applauded, admired and appreciated. Merely doing great acts of service for God (or others) isn't what God is looking for. He wants a heart that serves him and others without admiring itself in the process.

As an exercise in humility, pray for a meek heart, one that is glad to serve God and others in the smallest of ways. Then look around. Ask God for eyes to see the things he wants you to do. I find one of the hardest places to do this is in serving my family without acting as if I am doing them a great favor or need to have them notice and appreciate me. Learn to give of yourself with a gentleness and a spirit of humility you haven't had before. Oftentimes, as you perform the menial tasks, God shows you deeper things.

My friend Janet shared her story with me:

When my son had surgery, I had a few encounters with humility. I stepped away from my writing desk and appointment book and ran up and down our stairs a hundred or more times a day to tote the machines that would help him get well. To help him to the bathroom. To fix meals and bandages and bedding. To wipe his face and clean up his vomit.

I started into these tasks with a sense that it would somehow work me more quickly into holiness. But when I thought of those who do this work for most of their lives, I realized that my couple weeks' effort was really rather puny in the big picture of sanctification. And THAT realization, rather than the works themselves, I think, was what pleased God—not seeing how far I'd come, but how far I still had left to go.

Fénelon said, "It is enough for me to do what you want me to do. For this purpose I was created."[18] Ask God for this to be the prayer of your heart too.

Exercise Two: Practice Hidden Service

Another aspect of humble service is the quality of hiddenness. A servant's heart prefers to remain hidden—obscure, unknown. It is forgetful of self. Acts of service cry out to be noticed, applauded, appreciated, and acclaimed.

Richard Foster says, "Nothing *disciplines* the inordinate desires of the flesh like service, and nothing *transforms* the desires of the flesh like serving in hiddenness."[19] Jesus tells us that we are not to let the right hand know what the left hand is doing (Matthew 6:1-6). Serving without fanfare or recognition nurtures a humble heart.

We can practice this kind of service through intercessory prayer and giving. Praying for others is sacrificial. It requires our time (a precious commodity these days) and a willingness to prioritize another's needs on our agenda. In prayer, we do this quietly, without attention drawn to ourselves. Through prayer, we invest our time and energy serving the needs of others without their knowing or noticing.

Giving is another way of serving others, although it is fraught with temptations for self-glory. Peter instructed us to use our gifts to serve others (1 Peter 4:10). We may do that but hope glory will come back on us for doing so. Dave and Donna were extremely wealthy and had the gift of monetary giving. They regularly donated large sums of money to ministries and people in need. How did I know? They would tell me. It is hard to keep our service or giving for an audience of One. Anonymity isn't always possible, but when you can, practice hiddenness in your service.

Humility isn't the medicine that cures all of life's ills, but it does create an internal posture in which problems with God, problems with self, and problems with others can be corrected and healed. These interior disciplines of truth, submission, and service are essential in cultivating a humble heart so that we can experience the blessings of a life well lived.

Personal Application

This chapter contains a lifetime's worth of application opportunities. To not become overwhelmed, choose just one of the exercises in the section on truth, submission, or service, and make an action plan on how you will begin to practice it in your daily life.

The Secret to Great Relationships

Honey, it's not that I don't love you.
My problem is that I just love myself more.

ROBIN BOISVERT

Fog draped itself over the landscape like a thick down blanket. I wasn't familiar with the lay of the terrain along these particular back roads I had taken. A wrong turn, and I could land in a steep ditch or a swollen creek. Slowly I navigated my way home, thankful for the white lines painted along the center of the road. I knew if I kept my eyes glued to the lines, I would not steer into harm's way.

Later, when I was safely snuggled into my warm bed, the Lord reminded me that life is a lot like my experience in the fog. The path can get pretty murky at times, especially when we talk about which one leads to happiness, loving relationships, and personal well-being. If we're not committed to staying close to God and his Word, we can lose our way amid all the conflicting philosophies.

But even on a clear day, white lines are important. They are painted on a roadway for a purpose. They keep traffic orderly and flowing smoothly. White lines help people drive safely, prevent accidents, and protect drivers, passengers, and pedestrians from injuries.

While I was in the Philippines, one of my most memorable and harrowing experiences on the road occurred when I was traveling by automobile in Manila. The traffic was so congested and crowded that the road's white lines made no difference. Drivers, including mine, just ignored them. What would normally be three lanes of traffic somehow expanded to five. More than once I was tempted to roll down my window and see if I could touch the car next to ours. Motorists thought nothing of crossing over into opposing traffic to get ahead of the rest of the pack. Often I rode with my eyes tightly shut to keep from feeling terrified.

Like the Manila drivers I encountered, we often choose to ignore God's white lines. We want the freedom to do our own thing, go our own way, be our own boss, make our own happiness. But instead of life becoming better, more fulfilling, or satisfying, it becomes more confusing, chaotic. The guidelines God gives us in his Word are not to restrict us but to teach us what makes life work. He knows what is best, and it is only as we humble ourselves and yield to his plan that we will find our true happiness in this life and in the next.

In chapter 3 I offered a working definition of humility: *Humility is an accurate assessment of who we are and a heartfelt acknowledgment that anything good in us is a result of God's goodness in us. It is admitting that all we are that is admirable comes from God, and therefore he gets the praise and the glory. Genuine humility is always accompanied by an inner attitude of deep submission to the lordship of Christ and a detachment from the desire for personal praise or recognition. The outward manifestation of this inward change is an absence of self-consciousness and an attitude of self-forgetfulness that enables a person to love others and serve them with the love of Christ without asking, "What's in it for me?" or, "How am I doing?"*

We have learned how essential humility is to deepening our intimacy with God. Now it's time to look at how humility makes a difference and actually benefits the way we see and interact with ourselves and with others.

RELATIONSHIP WITH OUR SELF

It might seem rather odd to talk about a relationship with our self. In the truest sense, of course, that is impossible. However, as we've already seen, we do think about our self and talk to our self (whether in good ways or bad ways) about who we are, what we want, and what we need to be happy and satisfied with life. We interact with our self and others in ways that will either lead to growth and maturity or pain and misery. Anyone who has struggled over an important decision, for example, has experienced relationship with self as he or she explored all the possibilities and pitfalls that such a decision might bring. Therefore, it is helpful that we understand how humility enables the development of a truthful self-image and appropriate self-care.

Significance Versus Self-Importance or Worthlessness

Humility reminds us that life is not all about finding ourselves, loving ourselves, or satisfying ourselves. This truth opens the gateway that leads to a meaningful and purposeful life. The backdrop behind a strong sense of identity is the assurance that we are deeply loved—not by ourselves, but by God. We believe that he has created us for a purpose, and therefore no one is worthless. As we know God better and see ourselves in the light of God's Word, we understand how silly it is to be full of our own importance as well as how valuable our unique role in God's purpose is.

Paul wrote about our significance when he talked about the various gifts in the body of Christ and how each one is vital to the building up of one another. He didn't want us to think that because our role in the body may be less visible, it is less important. He wrote, "The eye cannot say to the hand, 'I don't need you!' And the head cannot say to the feet, 'I don't need you!' On the contrary, those parts of the body that seem to be weaker are indispensable, and the parts that we think are less honorable we treat with special honor." (See 1 Corinthians 12:12-31 for more of Paul's teaching on this subject.)

As in the human body, those parts that are unseen and less glamorous, like the liver or the kidneys, are actually more crucial to the body's overall health than the eyes and the ears. When we minimize our God-given gifts as insignificant or worthless, we don't see things truthfully. Our significance does not come from which gift or ability we have; rather, it comes from how those abilities function with others for the greater purpose of edifying the body of Christ. When we think our part doesn't matter, we miss the blessings that come when we live for his purposes and have an impact on others for all eternity (Ephesians 2:10).

On the other hand, Paul also cautioned us against puffing ourselves up with our own importance. He wrote, "If the whole body were an eye, where would the sense of hearing be? If the whole body were an ear, where would the sense of smell be? But in fact God has arranged the parts in the body, every one of them, just as he wanted them to be" (1 Corinthians 12:17-18).

When we are full of our own self-importance, we minimize the contributions that others make. We usually want people to notice what we are doing and to appreciate us. Often we feel disappointed or angry when we don't get the recognition or praise we deserve. Humility frees us from our inordinate self-consciousness and self-concern. As we forget ourselves we become free to grow joyfully into who God has made us as we serve a higher purpose than our own vainglory. Thus the entire concept of self-esteem becomes redefined from God's perspective. Our self-esteem is not poor because it is "low" (meaning worthless), but because it is "off base" (meaning not rightly aligned with God's view). Humility gives us an accurate lens from which to see ourselves.

Self-Acceptance Versus Inordinate Self-Love or Self-Hatred

Jennifer and Mike came for counseling because of depression and marital strife. Jennifer was unhappy and tried to express her feelings to her husband, but he responded in such a negative way that it scared her. Mike would get depressed, sulk, and say, "Yeah, I guess you married a loser. I'm a lousy husband, a terrible provider. You'd be better off without me." His remarks shut down any constructive communication in his marriage. Even worse, his posture hindered him from growing. Mike's sense of self was so fragile that he could not bear to hear anything negative about himself without becoming overwhelmed with anger, self-hatred, and self-pity. Dick Keyes cautioned:

> If your self-acceptance rests on maintaining an image of yourself as a nice, good person who never did anything wrong on purpose, then you cannot allow much truth into your field of vision. True self-acceptance is in stark contrast to this self-delusion. Self-acceptance does not survive honesty; it rests on it. The Christian is not someone who is so brave or thick-skinned that he can face the truth about himself unafraid;

rather he is a sinner who can face his sin because he has confidence that God has forgiven and accepted him in spite of it.[1]

Self-acceptance doesn't mean that you like everything you see; it means that you honestly see what is (Psalm 139). We accept the truth about ourselves, that we are a mixture of strong and weak, good and bad, naughty and nice. It is not healthy or humble to stay down in the dumps about the truth. Acceptance means that we learn not to hate or resent ourselves when confronted about our immature character or the sins displayed in our attitudes, thoughts, or behaviors. Rather than wallow in self-hatred and despair, we need to repent, take corrective action, and discipline ourselves in the ways of God so that we might become more like him.

Self-acceptance also allows us to celebrate and affirm God's gifts and good work in our lives, knowing that it is *of* him and *from* him we have these gifts and opportunities. Many people are miserable because they continually compare themselves to others. They feel inferior because they tell themselves that they don't measure up or that they are not as gifted as someone else. When I went to college, I thought of becoming a psychiatrist. But I came to accept that I did not have the intelligence to master the math and science required to get into medical school. I was disappointed, but instead of being angry and resenting my limits, I accepted them. Only from that place could I discover the strengths God had given me. Romano Guardini said: "The act of self-acceptance is the root of all things. I must agree to be the person who I am. Agree to have the qualifications which I have. Agree to live within the limitations set for me.... The clarity and the courageousness of this acceptance is the foundation of all existence."[2]

Godly Self-Care Versus Self-Admiration or Self-Indulgence

The Bible never says we should ignore ourselves completely. If we did that, we would not be good stewards of what God has entrusted to us. However, just like white lines are essential to road safety, God's Word provides the guidelines on what biblical self-love is supposed to look like. Humility enables us to care for ourselves properly without getting absorbed in ourselves, whether in morbid introspection, self-pity, or self-indulgence.

We Seek God in Our Lives

Humility teaches us that it is in our best interest to put God first and to take the time to know him, not only for what he provides (like wisdom and temporal and eternal blessings), but also for who he is. In his excellent book *Desiring God,* John Piper wrote:

> Christian Hedonism [pursuing God because it makes us
> happy] combats pride because it puts man in the category
> of an empty vessel beneath the fountain of God. It guards
> us from the presumption of trying to be God's benefactors.
> Philanthropists can boast. Welfare recipients can't. The primary
> experience of the Christian Hedonist is *need.* When a little,
> helpless child is being swept off his feet by the undercurrent on
> the beach, and his father catches him just in time, the child
> does not boast; he hugs.[3]

The psalms tell us to "Delight yourself in the LORD!" (Psalm 37:4). God says that he is our soul's joy and satisfaction (Psalm 21:6) and that following his ways leads to great joy (Psalm 19:8; 1 Peter 1:8).

Humble self-love realizes that our greatest pleasure isn't in self or in stuff; it is in God. Therefore, we pursue him with vigor. Piper also observed, "Our quest is not merely joy. It is joy *in* God. And there is no way for a creature to consciously manifest the infinite worth and beauty of God without delighting in him."[4]

We Seek God's Wisdom for Our Lives

God knows we all want to be happy, and he clearly tells us in his Word what will bring joy, contentment, and blessing to our lives. He also warns us that rebellion and unfaithfulness lead to sorrow, despair, and death (Psalm 68:6; Proverbs 13:15). Throughout the book of Proverbs, we learn that God says we will find good things as we love him and acquire wisdom in our lives. "He who gets wisdom loves his own soul; he who cherishes understanding prospers" (Proverbs 19:8). Lloyd Ogilvie defined wisdom as "a God-given ability to perceive people and situations with spiritual clarity."[5] Wisdom paints the white lines that help us navigate safely through those foggy philosophies, murky world-views, and cultural riptides so we will not meet our demise. Proverbs warns us that those who fail to find wisdom harm themselves (Proverbs 8:36).

For example, wisdom teaches us that pride doesn't make us happy; instead, it makes us and those all around us miserable. (See, for example, Proverbs 11:2; 13:10; 16:18-19; 17:7; 21:4; 29:23.) In *The Life of God in the Soul of Man,* Henry Scougal said:

> The proud and arrogant person is a trouble to all that converse
> with him, but most of all unto himself: every thing is enough
> to vex him; but scarce any thing sufficient to content and
> please him. He is ready to quarrel with every thing that falls
> out; as if he himself were such a considerable person that God

Almighty should do every thing to gratify him, and all the creatures of heaven and earth should wait upon him, and obey his will.[6]

I could relate to that proud man. At the grocery store recently I grumbled and complained to the store manager because everything I was looking for that particular day was out of stock. *Don't they realize I'm a busy person? I don't have time to come back or go to another store. How dare they not have what I need*—as if my needs and what I want are the most important things to consider! When I got to my car I was filled with sorrow over my pride. It's easier to believe I'm learning to be humble when no one disappoints me or angers me. Once again I had to repent and cry out for Jesus to show me his ways. Do you think that God was trying to teach me some wisdom in the form of patience and forbearance when the grocery store was out of all the things I wanted? Probably, but I failed the lesson the first time around. God always provides opportunities for me to learn his ways. I need his wisdom to see them.

James tells us that there are two kinds of wisdom: God's wisdom and worldly wisdom (James 3:13-17). Sometimes we waver in trusting God's wisdom. We aren't sure what will make us the happiest in life and are tempted to go with what feels good now. We yell at those with whom we're upset. We get divorced because we are desperately unhappy in our marriage. We have an affair because it feels so wonderful to have someone finally pay attention to us and our needs. We peek at pornography, loving the rush of excitement and titillation offered in the privacy of our own home. "But," Fénelon warned, "in spite of its dazzling, deceptively beautiful appearance, worldly wisdom has a fearsome flaw—*it brings death to all who take it as the rule by which they live.*"[7]

God's Word teaches us that we can only know what will make us the happiest when we look through the wide-angle lens of life and see the big picture. James wrote, "The wisdom that comes from heaven is first of all pure; then peace-loving, considerate, submissive, full of mercy and good fruit, impartial and sincere" (James 3:17). God also warns us what happens when we refuse to listen to his wisdom: "At the end of your life you will groan, when your flesh and body are spent. You will say, 'How I hated discipline! How my heart spurned correction! I would not obey my teachers or listen to my instructors. I have come to the brink of utter ruin in the midst of the whole assembly'" (Proverbs 5:11-14). What a terrible trade to make for a few moments of pleasure or relief.

We Will Correct and Discipline Ourselves

We live in a self-indulgent culture. Credit-card debt is skyrocketing because we have a hard time saying no to ourselves. After all, "We deserve it!" Obesity, sexual promiscuity, pornography, drug abuse, and alcoholism are at all-time highs. Not only do we tend to indulge our fleshly appetites, we also indulge our immature and sinful ways of thinking, feeling, and behaving. We sulk in self-pity, throw temper tantrums when we don't get our way, nurse angry and hateful thoughts, and wallow in our morbid self-analysis. When we feel unhappy or hurt, lonely or unloved, we wrongly believe that we will feel better if we indulge ourselves.

That is not true. People are more miserable and don't like themselves more than ever. The results of a self-indulgent psyche or lifestyle are not happiness and good self-esteem, but bondage. Thomas à Kempis observed, "Continual peace is with the humble, but in the heart of the proud is envy and frequent indignation."[8]

When we live by our temporary cravings and feelings instead of disciplining ourselves to live by what is true, good, or right, we will always get into trouble. For example, overeating may bring satisfaction in the moment, but we usually feel awful later, both physically and mentally. "Oh, I shouldn't have eaten so many cookies or all that pizza. I'm so mad at myself." We feel unhappy when we receive our credit-card bill after splurging on an extravagant vacation or present we could not afford and then have to spend the next five years paying for it. As a counselor I've sat with hundreds of hurting people who must daily live with the physical, emotional, and relational consequences of unrestrained sexual appetites, harsh tongues and tempers, undisciplined emotions, and wayward and untrue thoughts. When we indulge our sinful nature we don't feel better; we feel worse. God tells us one of the causes of self-hatred is ignoring discipline (Proverbs 15:32).

Earlier we learned that Mike had a problem hearing his wife's feelings about their relationship without sinking into shame and self-pity. However, when Mike began to open up and talk with Jennifer about some of the things that he didn't like, she defensively shot back, "You know I have a bad temper. I'm just being myself!" I asked her, "Jennifer, which self are you being? Your old self, with your sinful patterns, or your new self, created to be like Christ?" (Ephesians 4:24).

Jennifer thought that loving herself meant she could excuse sinful behavior under the guise of "being herself." As we learned, properly loving yourself doesn't mean you excuse yourself; rather you correct yourself so you can grow into the person God intends.

OUR RELATIONSHIP WITH OTHERS

We are called to be imitators of God and to live a life of love (Ephesians 5:1-2). Selflessness is an essential component of this command. Our humility before God should make a difference in the way we see and treat others. When pride and selfishness get in the way, we obscure Christ's image in us. People no longer see Jesus in us; they see us in us.

Relationship difficulties can bring out the best in us. They also often bring out the worst in us. It is in the context of relationships that most of our spiritual and emotional maturing takes place. For how do we learn to love sacrificially or to live selflessly if we are alone? We can't. It is in our daily interactions with others that our pride and selfishness, our fear of rejection or conflict and our excessive self-consciousness, our sinful behaviors and wrong thinking patterns are brought to light.[9] Our relationships often function like those little red tablets you get from the dentist to show you where you didn't brush your teeth correctly. I call them plaque finders. After brushing your teeth, you think all is well until you chew the red tablet. Then voilà— your teeth look like you've been drinking gallons of cherry Kool-Aid. The tablet exposed what had been there all along, but you didn't see it until the right circumstances made it obvious.

Our interactions with people are sort of like that. We think we have died to our pride, our selfishness, and then—*wham!* Our spouse doesn't appreciate that we've worked all day to please him or her. Our dog or our neighbor irritates us. The folks at church don't seem to pay enough attention to us. The grocery store doesn't have what we need, the bank has a long line, or our children give us a smart response. Watch what happens in you and to you when these things occur. Jesus tells us that it is "out of the overflow of his heart his mouth speaks" (Luke 6:45). What gushes out of our mouths in these moments reveals what is in our heart. Most often what is there is aligned with self-centered desires. We want to be noticed! We want our way! We want to be right! We want to be listened to or obeyed! We want to be catered to! We want to be first! We want what makes things better for us.

It is important to understand that these moments of exposure are for our good. They are not meant to shame us or propel us into self-hatred any more than finding plaque on our teeth is a sign that we should yank them all out or put a bag over our head. In fact, those red tablets are meant to show us the weaknesses in our brushing technique so we will learn to brush correctly, because accumulated plaque on our teeth leads to gum disease and tooth loss. In the same way, when our sins are exposed, it is not helpful to become angry and defensive or to slip into self-hatred. Instead, we need to be honest with ourselves so we can take corrective action. Otherwise, unconfessed pride and selfishness lead to broken relationships.

Pride and Selfishness Lead to Damaged Relationships

As a Christian counselor for more than twenty years, I could relate story after story of how the lack of humility and meekness led to pain, heartache, and shattered relationships. Our selfish, self-centered, and prideful attitudes play out in hundreds of different ways within a marriage, a family, a church, a neighborhood, a workplace, and anywhere that we interact with people. James asked, "What is the source of quarrels and conflicts among you?" (James 4:1, NASB). The bottom line? Selfishness and pride. (See James 4.) James presented a simple solution: "Submit yourselves" (verse 7) and "humble yourselves" (verse 10).

As we learned in chapter 8, submission isn't just for wives. All believers are called to submit to authority (1 Peter 2:13), to one another (Ephesians 5:21), and to God (James 4:7). Submission and humility go together like a hand in a glove. Paul tells us, "Do nothing out of selfish ambition or vain conceit, but in humility consider others better than yourselves. Each of you should look not only to your own interests, but also to the interests of others" (Philippians 2:3-4).

We usually have no problem looking out for our own interests; it's the interests of others that we struggle to consider as important as our own.

Ken loved the outdoors. His favorite kind of vacation was to pitch a tent in a place where he could hike and fish until dark. Carol, his wife, hated camping. She loved the beach, nice hotels, and restaurants. Every year they fought over their family vacation (among other things). Ken thought that since he worked hard all year, he deserved at least two weeks of the year to do the things he found fun and relaxing. Carol wanted time off from household duties and entertaining kids; to her, camping was more of the same, only harder. She wanted to eat out and relax by the pool.

As a counselor I'm often asked to mediate these kinds of standoffs in a marriage. They can be over vacations, how to spend the holidays, in-law struggles, parenting differences, financial goals and priorities— often under the guise of "We have a communication problem." Most of the time failure to be considerate of the other person's feelings and perspective—not poor communication—is the real issue. Each wants his or her own way!

Paul instructs us: "Do not use your freedom to indulge the sinful nature; rather, serve one another in love. The entire law is summed up in a single command: 'Love your neighbor as yourself.' If you keep on biting and devouring each other, watch out or you will be destroyed by each other" (Galatians 5:13-15). Catherine of Siena wisely observed: "And who is hurt by the offspring of your pride? Only your neighbors. For you harm them when your exalted opinion of yourself leads you to consider yourself superior and therefore to despise them. And if pride is in a position of authority, it gives birth to injustice and cruelty, and becomes a dealer in human flesh."[10]

Even when we're not blatant or conscious of our pride and selfishness, without humility, our heart is automatically oriented toward serving, defending, or protecting our self. We react defensively when we are criticized; if we were humble, we would take in the criticism and carefully consider its validity. Gary Thomas wrote: "One of Satan's favorite ploys to keep us from truth is to make us despise the messenger of truth."[11]

We refuse to apologize or ask for forgiveness, rationalizing our behavior or blaming circumstances or others for our own failures. We bristle when we are told to seek outside help, telling ourselves *we don't need it;* if we were humble, we would be more honest, allowing ourselves to be teachable. We hold on to grudges and past hurts. We nurse bad attitudes toward others because we deem them unworthy of our love, respect, or forgiveness. Humility reminds us that we, too, are unworthy of God's love, grace, and forgiveness; therefore, who are we to withhold mercy toward others?

A humble heart leads to healed relationships. Recently one of my clients shared with me a little note she received from one of her grandchildren. The child innocently said that she was scared to come over anymore because, as she wrote, "You're always mad, Grandma." Instead of reacting angrily or defensively, Grandma's proud heart broke. The gentle and loving honesty of her little granddaughter exposed the woman's longstanding angry and haughty spirit, and Grandma began to repent. Immediately she called her granddaughter, thanking her for her note, and assuring her that she would work on this problem so that her granddaughter would no longer be scared to visit. She boldly and humbly did something along the lines that Francis de Sales once suggested: "As soon as you see that you are guilty of a wrathful deed, correct the fault right away by an act of meekness toward the person you were angry with. It is a sovereign remedy against lying to contradict the untruth upon the spot as soon as we see we have told one. So also we must repair our anger instantly by a contrary act of meekness. Fresh wounds are quickest healed."[12]

Successful Relationships

Many years ago John Malloy wrote a popular book called *Dress for Success*. Malloy's premise was that our clothing gives people an important first impression of who we are. Therefore, if we want to be successful in business, it is crucial that we dress according to the impression that we wish to make. This concept did not originate with Malloy. God's Word tells us how to dress for success in our relationships. I especially like the way Eugene Peterson captured it in *The Message*. He wrote:

> Don't lie to one another. You're done with that old life. It's like a filthy set of ill-fitting clothes you've stripped off and put in the fire. Now you're dressed in a new wardrobe. Every item of your new way of life is custom-made by the Creator, with his label on it. All the old fashions are now obsolete. Words like Jewish and non-Jewish, religious and irreligious, insider and outsider, uncivilized and uncouth, slave and free, mean nothing. From now on everyone is defined by Christ, everyone is included in Christ.
>
> So, chosen by God for this new life of love, dress in the wardrobe God picked out for you: compassion, kindness, humility, quiet strength, discipline. Be even-tempered, content with second place, quick to forgive an offense. Forgive as quickly and completely as the Master forgave you. And regardless of what else you put on, wear love. It's your basic, all-purpose garment. Never be without it. (Colossians 3:10-14)

As our internal attitude about ourselves shifts from "me first" to "God first," we learn to love. There can be no authentic or lasting love for one another or for God without humility. Jesus raised the bar on loving others. He didn't merely command us to love our neighbor as ourselves. He said, "My command is this: Love each other as I have loved you. Greater love has no one than this, that he lay down his life for his friends" (John 15:12-13). We must love one another *more* than we love ourselves. We must love others as Jesus does.

I'm often asked, "How can I honor or love someone I don't respect?"

One of the reasons we struggle with understanding love is because our culture is in a fog regarding what genuine love is. We've learned about love from Hollywood and Harlequin, not from God's Word. Therefore, if we don't have that certain loving feeling, how can we love?[13] God's answer is this: We love with humility, meekness, and gentleness. Love cares about the other person's welfare and his or her good. Do you think Jesus loved us because he respected us? Neither is that a prerequisite for us to love as he has loved or to forgive as he forgives.

The apostle Paul wrote about what this kind of love looks like. In his well-known passage in 1 Corinthians 13 he explained: "Love is patient, love is kind. It does not envy, it does not boast, it is not proud. It is not rude, it is not self-seeking, it is not easily angered, it keeps no record of wrongs. Love does not delight in evil but rejoices with the truth. It always protects, always trusts, always hopes, always perseveres. Love never fails" (verses 4-8).

This kind of love is a giving love, not a taking love. Andrew Murray said, "Perfect love...forgets itself and finds its blessedness in blessing others, in bearing with them and honoring them, however weak they may be."[14]

Perhaps if Ken and Carol had practiced a selfless love in their marriage, their vacation plans, as well as other difficulties in their marriage, would not have resulted in so much conflict, with each fighting to get his or her own way. As they looked out for the best interests of each other instead of themselves, they might have found the joy of pleasing one another and the hidden blessing that is ours when we sacrifice without resentment in order to lovingly meet the needs of our spouse.

Paul also taught that "love does no harm to its neighbor" (Romans 13:10). What would our homes be like if we made it our commitment to do no harm to our spouse or children? What if we promised God we would do no harm to his body in the church or to anyone who considers us an example of what God is like? God's love is sacrificial. Selfless. Extravagant. Impossible for us to mirror perfectly—unless we empty ourselves of our own agenda of "What's in it for me?"

Imagine how different our home, our church, our community— our very life—would be if we, as God's children, chose:

- humility over pride
- servanthood over competition
- selflessness over selfishness
- compassion over contempt
- kindness over rudeness
- gentleness instead of harshness
- patience instead of anger
- forgiveness instead of bitterness
- self-control instead of self-indulgence

Then Christ's words would ring true, loud, and clear throughout our world: They will know you are Christians by your love for one another (John 13:35).

PERSONAL APPLICATION

Prayerfully journal how your pride and selfishness or perhaps even your morbid self-consciousness have hurt your relationships with others. Remember, honesty before God and before self is a prerequisite in order for humility to grow.

In your marriage _____

With your children _____

In the body of Christ _____

At work and with others _____

After you have been honest with yourself before God, humble yourself, and ask for forgiveness from those you have wounded.

The Joy of a Life Well Lived

Your purpose is not to be seen
or known or loved or admired or praised.
Your purpose is to see,
know, love, admire, and praise God.

GUIGO

As I contemplate what Jesus is showing me about humility, it is
tempting to feel overwhelmed. *It's so hard to be selfless. It is no
fun being a servant.* A small yet very persistent inner voice nags, *But
what about ME and MY needs?* The good news is that Jesus doesn't
model humility and teach it because it's merely good for us as his followers to learn. He directly links humility to our happiness and well-
being. It is critical that we understand how humbling ourselves not
only blesses God and blesses others—it blesses us.

Two Roads

Have you ever looked back and said, "If I had known then what I
know now, I would have _____"?

When we look for what really matters in life, sometimes the best perspective comes at the end. From that vantage point it is possible to look at the whole picture, where we see clearly enough to evaluate what's important and what's not. Everyone wants to have a life of peace, joy, and love and a life with a sense of purpose. In other words, a life well lived.

How we get there is the dilemma we all face.

Throughout this book we have been looking down two opposite paths. Both promise life, happiness, and satisfaction. One road is dense with the lush greenery of self-affirming, self-pleasing choices. Gigantic billboards pulsate with neon lights directing us to love ourselves, find ourselves, please ourselves, and satisfy ourselves. After all, we deserve it! The other road appears sparse, dusty, definitely less traveled. Rutted and hilly, its only remarkable feature is a roughly hewn cross scrawled with the message to deny yourself, lose yourself, humble yourself, and sacrifice yourself.

At first glance the lush path is more appealing, and many choose to walk in that direction, searching for what those big signs promise. But as we have learned, the way that is most appealing to our flesh is the one that leads to a sad and disappointing life in the long run. Travelers along that road might experience some temporary pleasure, but the end is heartache.

The Bible tells us about the lives of two different people—one in the Old Testament and one in the New Testament—who both chose to follow the lush path. Their stories are written from hindsight. If they were to speak to us today, they might begin their story with, "If I had known then what I know now, I would have made different choices."

Let's learn a lesson from their lives.

The Teacher from the Old Testament

The writer of Ecclesiastes wrote this book while looking back over his life. That is what gives it such poignant clarity. The author is unknown, but some Bible scholars think that King Solomon penned it.

Whoever the author, he was a man who had all of life's choices available to him. He was learned, wise, successful, confident, and powerful—all of the things that our world believes lead to a life well lived. What did he learn? First, he tried living for sensual pleasure, but that didn't bring any lasting satisfaction. Next he passionately pursued his work—still empty. Listen to what he wrote:

> I denied myself nothing my eyes desired;
>> I refused my heart no pleasure.
> My heart took delight in all my work,
>> and this was the reward for all my labor.
> Yet when I surveyed all that my hands had done
>> and what I had toiled to achieve,
> everything was meaningless, a chasing after the wind;
>> nothing was gained under the sun.
>
> (Ecclesiastes 2:10-11)

The writer then looked beyond his life and saw more meaninglessness, more nothingness. Money didn't help; it was never enough (5:10). He saw envy and injustice, strife and folly, and concluded that life is difficult and unfair even when you try to live right. Wisdom helps, but in the end sometimes it just isn't enough to understand God or his ways.

So what ultimately mattered? Was there anything worth living for? The teacher's words tell us what is important. He said we're to appreciate and value our relationships, because they are what bring joy and comfort (4:9-12; 9:9). He encouraged us to be purposeful in all we do (9:10), and he warned us to live our lives with the end in view because, he said, judgment comes to all. He concluded his observations simply by advising us to "fear God and keep his commandments, for this is the whole duty of man" (12:13).

The Rich Man from the New Testament

Jesus told the story of two men, a rich man who dressed in purple clothes and lived a luxurious life, and Lazarus, a hungry beggar covered with sores (see Luke 16:19-31). They both died. Angels carried Lazarus to Abraham's side, while the rich man found himself in hell. In this place, the man who lacked nothing in worldly goods surveyed his life lucidly.

In the account, the rich man asked to have Lazarus sent back to his father's house—to warn his family about what really mattered. Jesus replied, "If they do not listen to Moses and the Prophets, they will not be convinced even if someone rises from the dead" (verse 31). From hindsight the rich man realized that he had lived his life selfishly, purposelessly, and foolishly. Now he was paying the price for not living with the end in mind. If he had known then what he now knew, he would have made different choices. He longed to warn those who were still alive to rethink what life is all about.

Unlike these two men, we do not need to wait until we are at the end of our lives to see clearly. God shows us the end. We need only to think about what he has revealed and believe him in order to change the direction in which we're heading.

A Meaningful Life

With the end in view, what does make life worth living? What brings joy, contentment, satisfaction, and purpose? Calvin Miller wrote, "George MacDonald listed what he called three grand essentials— three things without which no meaningful life can be lived: someone to love, something to do, and something to hope for."[1]

Someone to Love

God is love, and he created us to love and be loved. It is absolutely essential for the human spirit to flourish. Without love, we shrivel up. However, in our self-oriented position, we have refused to love the one who deserves our adoration the most. Instead, we have substituted ourselves as the center of our lives and the object of our devotion.

Those who travel the lush path forsake a life well lived, because they aren't looking for someone to love; they are looking for someone to love *them*. They may flit from relationship to relationship because the person they were "in love with" no longer pleases them or satisfies them or meets their needs. In other words, *He or she doesn't love me as I want him (her) to anymore, so I must find someone else to love ME.* In addition to searching for someone to love them, they are working on loving themselves. Their love is self-consuming and self-oriented.

When we focus on loving ourselves, we miss God's best. Instead of loving God, our very source of life and goodness, we love other things that harm our relationship with God and others. For example, we love our way (James 4:1-3); we love being right (Luke 11:45-46); we love being first (Luke 14:8-11). We love the world (1 John 2:15). We love money (Luke 16:14; Hebrews 13:5). We love the praise of humankind (John 12:43). We love sin (John 3:19), and we love positions of status and authority (Matthew 23:6-7; Luke 11:43). God warns us about our other loves. He calls them idols. God is a jealous God. He is jealous of our love. When we love things or other people (including ourselves) more than we love him, we will forfeit our intimacy with him. He calls it spiritual adultery, and it breaks his heart (Ezekiel 6:9).

Sometimes we pretend to love God, but what we're really doing is using him as a means to get the other things that we love. We read, "Delight yourself in the LORD and he will give you the desires of your heart" (Psalm 37:4), and we interpret that to mean that if we give God some token attention, he will give us what we really long for. It's still all about us. We live as if God is here to serve us and make us happy. Humility changes that self-serving orientation. God wants the deepest desire of our heart to be to know him and our greatest joy to be in loving him, not in loving what he gives us.

Jesus warns us that who or what we love is crucial to our well-being, because he knows that what controls our heart controls us (Matthew 6:21). What we love orders our priorities, determines how we invest our resources of time, money, energy and talents, and tells us what's worth living for—and dying for.

For example, committed athletes give up some of their favorite foods and certain recreational activities to more fully devote themselves to training and practice for their sport. Why? Because they love their sport and want to excel. A mom or dad willingly gets up in the middle of the night to feed and comfort a crying child, often sacrificing much-needed sleep to show loving care. This same principle is true even when we love bad things or things that we know are not good for us. For instance, those who love drugs have been known to forsake a good job, friends, and even a spouse because of the desire to get high. The love for drugs has become their all-consuming passion. Hosea lamented that Israel "became as vile as the thing that they loved" (Hosea 9:10). What we love changes us. We become like the object of our love.

Please don't misunderstand me. Loving our children, other people, and wholesome activities aren't wrong or bad for us. God wants us to love extravagantly, even those who are considered our enemies (Luke 6:27). However, as Oswald Chambers warned us: "The great enemy of the life of faith in God is not sin, but the good which is not good enough."[2] Many of us love good things, things that are not inherently sinful or evil, yet this isn't enough for a life well lived.

God says that he is the only one worthy of our fullest love, greatest attention, and deepest devotion. In both the Old and New Testaments he repeatedly commands us to love him with everything that is in us—all of our heart, mind, soul, and strength. God knows that the most important and satisfying love relationship we can possibly have is not with another human being but with God.

As our Creator, God has designed our heart to find its fulfillment and satisfaction in loving him. Thomas à Kempis counseled, "You ought to leave your beloved for your Beloved…for Jesus will be loved above all things. The love of things created is deceitful and inconstant; the love of Jesus is faithful and persevering. He who cleaves unto a creature shall fall with that which is subject to fall; he who embraces Jesus shall be made strong forever."[3]

God knows how fickle the human heart is. That's why he clearly commands us to love him first and foremost. He knows that only when we love him the most will we find our soul's true satisfaction. Bernard of Clairvaux observed:

God alone can satisfy our desires. A man with a lovely wife
may still look lustfully at an attractive woman. A well-dressed

person wants more expensive clothes. The rich envy the richer. You can find people who already own much property and have many possessions, still striving, day in and day out, to add another field to their estates. They have a restless ambition for promotion and honors.

It is not very intelligent to desire what can never satisfy. While enjoying wealth, you keep searching for something you still lack. You run back and forth from one pleasure to another, becoming tired, but never satisfied. Who can own everything? Whatever you cling to, you are surely going to lose one day. You are running down a twisting road and you will die before you reach the end of it.

Eventually, we will come to say to God, "Whom have I in heaven but you? And earth has nothing I desire besides you" (Psalm 73:25). Anything else is doomed to failure. Life is too short, strength too limited, competition too fierce. The long road wears us out.[4]

God knows it is in our absolute best interest for us to love him. Real and lasting joy is found in the Life (John 14:6), not in life. That's why he commands us to love *him,* not what he does for us. Loving God leads us to a deeper intimacy with him (John 14:21,23), to peace (John 14:27), and joy (John 15:11). Our love for God also empowers us to humble ourselves, obey him, and love others.

Something to Do

Jesus asked Peter three times if he loved him (John 21:15-17). Only after Peter repeatedly declared his love for Christ did Jesus tell him the next part of what makes life meaningful—something to do. Jesus gave

Peter a purpose to live for, something to do that would matter for all of eternity, an opportunity to lead a life well lived. When our heart is ignited with the flames of passion for God, our life takes on new meaning, and we find purpose and value. We are delighted in life, whatever it holds, because we are participating with God in the work of redemption.

Oftentimes we think that what we are supposed to do has to be big and bold in order for it to be significant. Anna was a multitalented woman who felt like she was wandering in circles. She said, "Leslie, I have no goals. I try to get through the chores and tasks of each day, taking care of kids, homework, and household responsibilities. There's no time for anything significant or meaningful." I asked her if she were to die next week, what regrets would she have? She thought for a moment and then said, "I'd regret that I didn't savor more moments now. I'm always wishing I could be finished so I could move on to more important things." When I asked Anna what were those important things she said, "Spending time with my family, like riding bikes, having a picnic, and enjoying a walk. But I never have enough time to do that because I'm too busy doing my chores."

Anna may need more balance and recreation in her life, but she is losing sight of the important work she is doing. She values time spent with her children but is only seeing the fun times as significant. "Anna," I probed, "what is the difference between savoring the time with your kids while riding bikes and feeling hassled with the kids during homework?" She looked up with a flash of insight and said, "Just my attitude! Maybe what I'm doing *is* important and significant *all the time,* but I didn't see it before." Oswald Chambers reminds us that "it is not the work we do for God that keeps us fresh; it is the work we allow God to do through us."[5]

Nicholas Herman was a middle-aged cook for the Order of the

Carmelites, a monastery in France. In the mundane, ordinary, daily tasks, Brother Lawrence (as he came to be called) practiced the presence of God in a powerful way. Brother Lawrence was content and satisfied doing what God asked him to do: cooking and cleaning up after others. Little did he comprehend the significant impact his faithful service and keen observations on living an ordinary life by faith would have on innumerable Christians for generations to come. His thoughts and casual conversations as well as some sparse notes and letters were collected by Abbé Joseph de Beaufort and published for others to read in the book *Practicing the Presence of God.* This little book has been read and loved by believers for hundreds of years.

In 1990 the president of Columbia Bible College (now Columbia International University) resigned in order to care for his ailing wife, Muriel, who had Alzheimer's. Some might look at Dr. McQuilkin's decision as foolish. After all, he was doing God's work at the college and had worldwide impact and international respect. Yet God ordained something new for him to do—to be the servant of one. His faithfulness, his commitment to his marriage vows, and his love for his ailing wife shine like a beacon in a plastic world of empty promises and broken relationships. Perhaps that work is the most significant he's ever done. When we live for God, loving him first, we consent to his plan for us, for we know we have important work to do. Calvin Miller said, "It is better to live a decade and know why we are alive than to live a century without any clue."[6]

Paul tells us that we are "God's workmanship, created in Christ Jesus to do good works, which God prepared in advance for us to do" (Ephesians 2:10). The word *workmanship* in the Greek means "poem." Through life's circumstances, God creates a movement to our lives that pulsates with eternal significance. Our unique dance with God becomes deeply satisfying as we yield ourselves to his rhythm.

Something to Hope For

Everyone needs something to hope in and hope for. Just like we can love the wrong things and invest our lives in pursuits that, in the end, won't matter, we can put our hope in things that are false, things that have no real substance and that lead to disappointment and heartache.

Katie grew up in an alcoholic family with six siblings. Part of what kept her sane during those tumultuous childhood years was the hope that when she grew up she would have the perfect life and perfect family. Today Katie battles depression and a sense of futility, not only because of her difficult childhood, but because what she hoped for isn't a reality. Even as an adult, Katie finds that life is hard and far from her hope of a perfect existence.

Dave came in to see me because his wife of six years "suddenly decided she didn't want to be married anymore," as he put it. After probing a bit, I discovered his wife hadn't made such a sudden decision after all. It was that Dave was hoping that she would "grow up and get over her whining about things." In the meantime, Dave tuned out his wife's increasing dissatisfaction with their marital relationship.

The hope God gives us isn't like the unrealistic hope in which Dave or Katie put their trust. God gives real hope, hope in something of substance, something that helps us face the pain of reality in a courageous way. True hope helps us persevere in the midst of hardship and difficulties rather than avoid them. Hope gives us the ability to see beyond the moment to something greater. The dictionary defines hope this way: "To cherish a desire with anticipation; a desire accompanied by expectation of or belief in fulfillment."[7]

As God's children, what desire can we cherish with eager anticipation? What can we expect to be fulfilled even in the most trying of situations? What can we hope for in order to experience contentment, a heart at rest, and a life well lived?

First, we have great hope and assurance in the character of God. The writer of Hebrews reminds us that God doesn't change and that God doesn't lie (Hebrews 6:18-19). This hope in the unfailing character of God provides an anchor for our souls. He is good, and when we choose to believe that, we have a stronghold "in times of trouble" (Nahum 1:7). God is not only good, but he is in control. Life is not an accident, nor is it haphazard. We believe that everything that happens to us has meaning and purpose, even if we don't understand at the time what that purpose is. The psalmist affirms this hope when he declares, "You are good, and what you do is good" (Psalm 119:68), even in the midst of affliction.

Another hope that God provides is an assurance that something good comes out of our suffering. We live in a world that sees suffering as a bad thing. Hope to the world mostly exists in the form of wishful thinking—*I hope this is over soon.* Although most of us may feel that way too, we have a hope that takes us beyond the desire for relief. God gives Christians a promise that something good comes out of our suffering, not just good for God or for other people, but good for us. Paul says that we are empowered to rejoice in our sufferings "because we know that suffering produces perseverance; perseverance, character; and character, hope. And hope does not disappoint us, because God has poured out his love into our hearts by the Holy Spirit, whom he has given us" (Romans 5:3-5). Paul also tells us that God will use everything in our lives for our good, which is to conform us to the image of Christ (Romans 8:28-29). Thus we know that our suffering is not meaningless or purposeless in this life or the next.

When all is said and done, life is hard. For some, the pain of life is almost unbearable. Even while on earth we get tastes of hell. The hope that sustains us in the midst of hell on earth is the hope of heaven. We believe Jesus when he said he was going to prepare a place for us (John 14:2) and would someday bring us home. In the midst of great hardship, Paul expressed hope in the eternal reality when he said, "Therefore we do not lose heart. Though outwardly we are wasting away, yet inwardly we are being renewed day by day. For our light and momentary troubles are achieving for us an eternal glory that far outweighs them all. So we fix our eyes not on what is seen, but on what is unseen. For what is seen is temporary, but what is unseen is eternal" (2 Corinthians 4:16-18). Later on he continued to express hope in heaven when he said, "Meanwhile we groan, longing to be clothed with our heavenly dwelling" (2 Corinthians 5:2).

Willie Peat, his wife, Helen, and their two daughters were missionaries in China in the early 1900s. They were captured and sentenced to death for their faith. In his last letter, Willie wrote his mother and uncle these words:

> The soldiers are just on us, and I have only time to say "Goodbye" to you all. We shall soon be with Christ, which is very far better for us. We can only now be sorry for you who are left behind and our dear native Christians.
>
> Goodbye! At longest it is only "til He come." We rejoice that we are made partakers of the sufferings of Christ, that when His glory shall be revealed we may "rejoice also with exceeding joy."

Helen added, "Our Father is with us and we go to Him, and trust to see you all before His face, to be forever together with Him."[8]

Hope in God's unchanging character, God's eternal plan, and the reality of heaven gave Willie and Helen Peat the courage to face an ugly death with faith and dignity. They knew their earthly life was coming to an end, and they knew with unwavering certainty they had lived well.

Ponder a few of the blessings hope in God brings us:

Find rest, O my soul, in God alone;
  my hope comes from him. (Psalm 62:5)

The LORD delights in those who fear him,
  who put their hope in his unfailing love.
                                  (Psalm 147:11)

But those who hope in the LORD
  will renew their strength.
They will soar on wings like eagles;
  they will run and not grow weary,
  they will walk and not be faint. (Isaiah 40:31)

Be joyful in hope, patient in affliction, faithful in prayer.
                                  (Romans 12:12)

May the God of hope fill you with all joy and peace as you trust in him, so that you may overflow with hope by the power of the Holy Spirit. (Romans 15:13)

Command those who are rich in this present world not to be arrogant nor to put their hope in wealth, which is so uncertain, but to put their hope in God, who richly provides us with everything for our enjoyment. (1 Timothy 6:17)

Thomas à Kempis counseled: "It is vanity to wish to live long, and to be careless to live well."[9] God's Word lights the way to a meaningful life: "He has showed you, O man, what is good. And what does the LORD require of you? To act justly and to love mercy and to walk humbly with your God" (Micah 6:8). Humility is foundational to a life well lived. It helps us recognize our dependence upon God for everything that is good and to appreciate all he does for us. Humility frees us from ourselves and enables us to use our gifts and abilities for eternal significance.

Selflessness is the only path that leads to lasting joy, contentment, peace, satisfaction with life, and genuine happiness. "The fruit of righteousness will be peace; the effect of righteousness will be quietness and confidence forever" (Isaiah 32:17). As we learn to walk in God's way, we will discover how wonderful it feels to be able to live in the freedom of our true self instead of in bondage to the false self we have created.

Two roads promise us the good life. Only one of those roads takes us there. The psalmist tells us which path to take: "You have made known to me the path of life; you will fill me with joy in your presence; with eternal pleasures at your right hand" (Psalm 16:11). I pray that you have the courage to walk in the way of selflessness. As you do, you will be delighted to find the enduring joy of a satisfied soul.

MAN'S GREAT END

Lord of all Being,
There is one thing that deserves my greatest care,
    that calls forth my ardent desires,
That is, that I may answer the great end for which I am
       made—

to glorify thee who has given me being,
and to do all the good I can for my fellow men;
Verily life is not worth having
if it be not improved for this noble purpose.
Yet, Lord, how little is this the thought of mankind!
Most men seem to live for themselves,
without much or any regard for thy glory,
or for the good of others;
They earnestly desire and eagerly pursue
the riches, honours, pleasures of this life,
as if they supposed that wealth, greatness, merriment,
could make their immortal souls happy;
But, alas, what false delusive dreams are these!
And how miserable ere long will those be that sleep in them,
for all our happiness consists in loving thee,
and being holy as thou art holy.

O may I never fall into the tempers and vanities,
the sensuality and folly of the present world!
It is a place of inexpressible sorrow, a vast empty nothingness;
Time is a moment, a vapour,
and all its enjoyments are empty bubbles,
fleeting blasts of wind,
from which nothing satisfactory can be derived;
Give me grace always to keep in covenant with thee,
and to reject as delusion a great name here or hereafter,
together with all sinful pleasures or profits.
Help me to know continually
that there can be no true happiness,

no fulfilling of thy purpose for me,
apart from a life lived in and for the Son of thy love.[10]

—*Valley of Vision*

PERSONAL APPLICATION

We tend to look for what God can do for us instead of what we can do for God. Our orientation is self-serving and self-seeking. Humbly thank God today that he has already done everything that you need. He has loved you, forgiven you, and given you his Holy Spirit to live inside of you. Now begin to ask God what you can do for him.

Can I suffer for you?

Can I love the unlovely for you?

Can I bear reproach for you?

Can I minister a cup of cold water for you?

Can I serve others for you?

Can I live for you?

Can I die for you?

Lord, it makes me happy to make you happy. That is my heart's true desire.

Study and Discussion Guide

Chapter One: Our Perilous Pursuit of Self

1. What's your reaction to the statement: "Perhaps our difficulties in life occur, not because we don't think highly *enough* of ourselves, but because we think *too highly* and *too much* of ourselves. Our problems in life usually don't stem from loving *ourselves* too little, but of *loving others and God* too little and ourselves too much." Do you agree? disagree? Explain your thoughts.

2. What comes to mind when you think of humility? Do you think the world values this virtue? In what ways do you think the church values or disregards humility?

3. In what ways have Christians bought into the world's philosophy that we must love ourselves before we can love others?

4. Chuck Colson comments, "This not-so-magnificent obsession to 'find ourselves' has spawned a whole set of counterfeit values; we worship fame, success, materialism, and celebrity. We want to 'live for success' as we 'look out for number one,' and we don't mind 'winning through intimidation.'"[1] Do you agree or disagree with Colson's analysis? How have these

false values influenced your thinking and your feelings about yourself?

5. Read 1 Corinthians 1:25-31. What does Paul's idea that God uses the "weak things of the world to shame the strong" have to do with our pursuit of self-love versus the selflessness of humility?

6. A. W. Tozer observed, "The labor of self-love is a heavy one."[2] What do you think he meant by this statement?

7. Read 2 Timothy 3:2-4. Paul tells us that people will be lovers of _____, lovers of _____, lovers of _____, rather than lovers of God. How have you seen this mind-set in the world? in the church? What do you love other than God or more than God?

8. What is the most helpful thing you have gleaned from this chapter? How might you apply it to your life?

Chapter Two: The Happiness Paradox

1. How does living for self apart from God degrade us?

2. Read Deuteronomy 30:11-20; Isaiah 30; and Jeremiah 7:23-24. What does God say are the consequences of going one's own way?

3. How would you define happiness? What does it take to find it?

4. How have you understood the Christian concept of "dying to self" in the past? Identify points in this chapter that helped you to see this concept in a fresh way.

5. In what ways do you struggle with self-sufficiency and independence from God?

6. The Bible says that when we are self-sufficient we have a tendency to forget God. Has that happened in your life when things are going smoothly? How can you prevent it from happening in the future?

7. How has self-righteousness kept you from deepening your relationship with God and with others?

8. Excessive self-consciousness and morbid introspection are subtle forms of pride. In what ways do you see yourself or others falling into this pattern in your life? What steps might you take to die to this habit?

9. Samson is an example of self-centered self-indulgence. In what ways do you use your abilities or gifts for selfish purposes? In what ways can you begin to use them for the benefit of others and for God's glory?

Chapter Three: Humility: What Is It, and Why Do We Avoid It?

1. What is your emotional response to hymns that describe us as worms or wretches? Do you agree that we have disdained

the virtue of humility because of our emphasis on having good self-esteem? Explain.

2. Reread the definitions of humility at the beginning of the chapter (pages 41-42). Do you agree or disagree with them? Why or why not? Are there any things you might add or change?

3. In describing humility, William Law wrote, "This virtue is so essential to the right state of our souls, that there is no pretending to a reasonable or pious life without it. We may as well think to see without eyes, or live without breath, as to live in the spirit of religion without the spirit of humility."[3] Why do you think some Christians view humility as optional?

4. Can a person grow as a Christian without humility? Why or why not?

5. Do you allow God's Word to describe and define you? Or do you allow your past, your upbringing, or our culture's values to determine your worth and your purpose?

6. Reread what God says about who you are. Compare what God says to what you have believed and thought. When your thoughts and feelings are contrary to God's Word, who wins? What are some of the lies you have bought into regarding self-esteem, self-love, and humility? Make a plan this week to challenge these lies with the truth of what God says.

Each time you are confronted with the lie, remind yourself
of the truth. This is the process of renewing our minds that
Paul speaks of in Romans 12:2.

7. What do you think you need to be happy and find joy
   in life?

8. What was the most helpful thing to you as you read
   this chapter? How might you begin to apply it to
   your life?

Chapter Four: Humility's Impostors

1. As you read this chapter, did anything surprise you? Explain
   what and why. Did you disagree with or find any particular
   idea difficult to accept? Which? Why?

2. How might you begin to think differently than you have in
   the past when you feel self-consciousness, shame, or self-
   hatred? What important biblical truths could you recall to
   help yourself at those times?

3. Francis de Sales said, "One of the best exercises in meekness
   we can perform is when the subject is in ourselves. We
   must not fret over our own imperfections."[4] In what way
   have you fretted over your weaknesses or flaws, imperfections or sins? Begin to confess this as sin (wounded
   pride) and ask God to teach you how to see yourself
   rightly.

4. Read through the parable of the talents in Matthew 25:14-30. How did fear of failure keep this man from using his gift in a wise way? Think about ways you might be hiding your talent(s) out of fear of failure.

5. Describe some specific ways that you have been "snared" by the fear of man (Proverbs 29:25), such as fear of rejection or the fear of disapproval. Journalize or share them with the group and ponder what you might begin to do differently when these snares come up again.

6. Do you agree with the statement, "True humility should free us from all preoccupation with ourselves, whereas a low self-opinion tends to focus our attention on ourselves?" Why or why not?

7. Describe an experience where you felt shame. What else did you feel? What did you think? What did you do? How might reading this chapter help you process shame differently?

8. Read 2 Corinthians 7:8-11. What is the difference between godly sorrow and worldly sorrow? What are the end results of each?

Chapter Five: Jesus: Our Example of Selflessness

1. Recall a time when you were humiliated. What happened? How did you feel? What did you do? Did it lead to humility or something else?

2. How does your pride keep you from learning from Christ?
   Are you open to correction from the Holy Spirit? God's
   Word? God's people?

3. Do you agree that humility begins with a choice? How
   have you chosen to lower or elevate yourself in the past?

4. How does your pride keep you from lowering yourself in
   relationship to your spouse? your coworkers? your children?
   other believers?

5. How do you handle being on the receiving end of service?
   Are you able to humble yourself and accept it, or do you
   refuse help?

6. What is the difference between feeling small and feeling
   worthless?

7. In what ways have you misused your authority and lacked
   humility with others? (Think of everyday relationships
   such as boss-worker, parent-child, husband-wife, pastor-
   parishioner, elder–lay person.)

8. What was the most important concept you learned from this
   chapter?

Chapter Six: The Fear of God Leads to Humility

1. How have you understood the fear of the Lord in the past?
   How important has it been to your relationship with God?

2. Gary Thomas wrote, "The twin pillars of a truly Christian spirituality are realizing our own lowliness and God's greatness."[5] How do you think these two outlooks work to encourage humility?

3. Read Psalm 139:17-18 and Isaiah 40:12-17. What has most deeply impressed you? Has it been God or other things?

4. Read Leviticus 10:1-3. How do believers show irreverence or disrespect for God today?

5. How might we learn to fear the Lord? Deuteronomy 17:19-20 speaks of the importance of learning this in our relationship with God.

6. How does the fear of the Lord unlock the treasure spoken of in Isaiah 33:5-6?

7. Read the following verses and look for some of the blessings and benefits of fearing God. Exodus 20:20; Psalms 25:9,12,14; 33:18; 34:8; 128:1; 147:11; Proverbs 1:7; 22:4; Jeremiah 2:19; 32:40; and Luke 1:50. How have you experienced these blessings in your life?

8. What was the most important thing God spoke to you about as you read this chapter?

Chapter Seven: Are You a Fan or a Friend?

1. What is your understanding of God's unconditional love? Do you agree that although God's love for us is undeserved, it does not automatically guarantee a relationship with him? Why or why not?

2. What are the important ingredients of a good marriage that would also hold true for our relationship with God?

3. Charles Spurgeon said: "Divine fellowship is never bestowed on haughty, high-minded sinners. The Lord respects the lowly and visits the contrite in heart, but the lofty are an abomination to Him."[6] Why do you think God hates pride so much?

4. How does pride manifest itself in your life and in your relationship with God? Is it overt or subtle?

5. Read Matthew 4:17; Mark 1:15; and Luke 13:5. Jesus says we must repent. What comes to mind when you think about repentance?

6. Is it ever difficult to admit your neediness to Jesus? How about to others? Why?

7. Can a person have a relationship with Jesus as Savior but not as Lord? Why or why not?

8. As you read this chapter, what stood out as the most important thing God was showing you? In what way can you begin to apply that truth to your life this week?

Chapter Eight: Growing in Selflessness

1. What most impressed you as you read this chapter?

2. Do you agree that there are things we must do to nurture humility in our heart? How have you done this in the past?

3. Francis de Sales said, "When attacked by some vice we must practice the contrary virtue as much as we can and refer all the others to it.... Thus if assaulted by pride or anger, I must devote and direct all my actions to humility and meekness."[7] When you are assaulted by your pride or anger, what might you do?

4. Have you been committed to truth with yourself? others? God? Read James 1:22-25. In what ways have you deceived yourself? When God shows you the truth about himself, about a relationship you're in, or about your own heart, do you act upon it, or do you "forget" and never deal with it?

5. How has this hindered your relationship with God or with others?

6. How have you understood submission in the past? Do you agree that all believers must learn submission? How have you practiced voluntary submission with others?

7. In what ways have you found genuine service difficult? Why?

8. How has practicing truth, submission, and service brought joy or happiness to your life?

Chapter Nine: The Secret to Great Relationships

1. "The backdrop behind a strong sense of identity is the assurance that we are loved—not by ourselves, but by God." How do problems with self-image and self-esteem become corrected when we learn to believe in and rest in the love of God?

2. Do you ever struggle with feeling worthless? Read 1 Corinthians 12:12-31. God has created you for a purpose and given you gifts and abilities to serve him and others. What are some of your gifts and talents?

3. In what ways have you struggled to accept yourself? Do you find it harder the more truthfully you look at yourself? How might the information in this chapter be helpful to you in learning to accept yourself in the future?

4. Whose wisdom do you most depend on—God's or the world's? God's Word defines self-love one way, the world another. Biblical self-love involves seeking God in our lives, acquiring and applying his wisdom to our life, and correcting and disciplining ourselves when necessary. Do you agree with this concept? In what ways do you struggle to apply

these things in your life? Is your self-love a more indulgent, self-justifying, or self-centered kind of love?

5. When you are in a disagreement with someone, what typically comes out of your mouth—blessings or curses? Read Luke 6:45. Jesus tells us that our speech reveals what is in our heart. What is going on in your heart during a conflict?

6. How have pride and selfishness hurt your relationships? Do you take responsibility for these sins and confess them, or do you blame others and make excuses for yourself?

7. The author states that humility and submission go together like a hand and glove. In what instances do you find submitting to others particularly difficult? Do you think your pride has something to do with it? How might you purposefully lower yourself to be more tolerant, forbearing, loving, forgiving, or patient?

8. Do you agree with the statement that humility is the secret of great relationships? Can you think of a more important character quality necessary for positive interaction with others?

Chapter Ten: The Joy of a Life Well Lived

1. Have you ever known anyone who was facing death? What did they regret? What did they teach you was important in life?

2. Do you live your life with the end in mind? Read Psalm 90:12. How do we live numbering our days?

3. Read Proverbs 21:21. What are we to pursue to find life, prosperity, and honor? What do we tend to pursue instead, and what do we find?

4. Read Job 27:13–28:28. What is the view from the end, and according to Job, what is important?

5. Do you agree with George MacDonald that a life well lived consists of someone to love, something to do, and something to hope for? Can you think of anything else that would be important to having a meaningful life?

6. What do you see as your reason for being here? How are you impacting eternity? Is that purpose in your mind as you as you live each day?

7. Which road do you tend to spend the most time on—the lush path or the sparse road? What steps might you take to walk more faithfully along the selfless path?

8. How does a life well lived bring joy to your heart? Are there other things that bring you joy and a sense of satisfaction?

Notes

1. Lois M. Miles, "How Blessed You Are." Used by permission.

Introduction

1. Thomas à Kempis, *Imitation of Christ* (Uhrichsville, Ohio: Barbour, 1984), 113.

Chapter One: Our Perilous Pursuit of Self

1. Nathaniel Branden, "In Defense of Self," *Association for Humanistic Psychology Perspectives* (August-September 1984): 12-3, quoted in Robyn M. Dawes, "The Social Usefulness of Self-Esteem: A Skeptical View," *The Harvard Mental Health Letter* 15, no. 4 (1998): 4.
2. John Piper, *Desiring God: Meditations of a Christian Hedonist* (Portland, Oreg.: Multnomah, 1986), 255.
3. Thomas à Kempis, *Imitation of Christ* (Uhrichsville, Ohio: Barbour, 1984), 55.
4. Blaise Pascal quoted in James M. Houston, *Mind on Fire: A Faith for the Skeptical and Indifferent* (Minneapolis: Bethany, 1997), 108.
5. Dawes, "The Social Usefulness of Self-Esteem," 4.
6. Brad J. Bushman and Roy F. Baumeister, "Threatened Egotism, Narcissism, Self-Esteem, and Direct and Displaced Aggression: Does Self-Love or Self-Hate Lead to Violence?" *The American Psychological Association Journal of Personality and Social Psychology* 75, no. 1 (1998): 219.

7. Oswald Chambers, *Devotions for a Deeper Life* (Grand Rapids: Zondervan, 1986), 79.

8. Paul C. Vitz, *Psychology As Religion* (Grand Rapids: Eerdmans, 1986), 91.

9. C. S. Lewis, *The Weight of Glory* (Grand Rapids: Eerdmans, 1949), 2.

Chapter Two: The Happiness Paradox

1. Charles Haddon Spurgeon, *Morning and Evening* (Peabody, Mass.: Hendrickson, 1995), 8.

2. Nathaniel Branden, *The Psychology of Self-Esteem* (Los Angeles: Nash Publishing, 1969), 235.

3. Martin Lloyd-Jones, *Studies in the Sermon on the Mount* (Grand Rapids: Eerdmans, 1959-60), 50.

4. *NIV Study Bible* (Grand Rapids: Zondervan, 1995), note on Mark 8:34.

5. William Law, *A Serious Call to a Devout and Holy Life* (Grand Rapids: Baker, 1977), 193.

6. Oswald Chambers, *Devotions for a Deeper Life* (Grand Rapids: Zondervan, 1986), 32.

7. François Fénelon, *Meditations on the Heart of God* (Brewster, Mass.: Paraclete Press, 1997), 142.

8. François Fénelon, *Talking with God* (Brewster, Mass.: Paraclete Press, 1997), 72.

9. Gary Thomas, *Seeking the Face of God* (Nashville: Nelson, 1994), 73.

10. Calvin Miller, *Into the Depths of God* (Minneapolis: Bethany, 2000), 107.

11. Andrew Murray, *Humility* (Gainsville, Fla.: Bridge-Logos Publishers, 2000), 36.

12. Oswald Chambers, *My Utmost for His Highest* (1935; reprint, Uhrichsville, Ohio: Barbour, 1963), 28.

13. Peggy Anderson, comp., *Great Quotes from Great Women* (Lombard, Ill.: Celebrating Excellence Publishing, 1992), 10.

14. Chambers, *My Utmost for His Highest*, 47.

Chapter Three: Humility:
What Is It, and Why Do We Avoid It?

1. John Piper, *Desiring God: Meditations of a Christian Hedonist* (Portland, Oreg.: Multnomah, 1986), 251.

2. Paul C. Vitz, *Psychology As Religion* (Grand Rapids: Eerdmans, 1986), 72.

3. Calvin Miller, *Into the Depths of God* (Minneapolis: Bethany, 2000), 56.

4. D. Stuart Briscoe, *The Communicators Commentary on Romans* (Waco, Tex.: Word, 1982), 13.

5. Larry Crabb, "When Elephants Dance," *Christian Counseling Today* 10, no. 1 (2002): 48.

6. Andrew Murray, *Humility* (Gainsville, Fla.: Bridge-Logos Publishers, 2000), 4.

7. François Fénelon, *Christian Perfection*, trans. Mildred Whitney Stillman (Minneapolis: Bethany, 1975), 206

8. Gary Thomas, *The Glorious Pursuit: Embracing the Virtues of Christ* (Colorado Springs: NavPress, 1998), 59.

9. Henry Nouwen, *Life of the Beloved: Spiritual Living in a Secular World* (New York: Crossroad, 1992), 49.

10. John Bevere, *The Fear of the Lord: Discover the Key to Intimately Knowing God* (Orlando: Creation House, 1997), 35.

11. Some of these ideas have been generated from Andrew Murray's excellent book *Humility.*

12. Bernard of Clairvaux, *On Loving God,* quoted in Bernard Bangley, *Near to the Heart of God* (Wheaton: Harold Shaw, 1998), August 2.

13. James M. Houston, *Mind on Fire: A Faith for the Skeptical and Indifferent* (Minneapolis: Bethany, 1997), 66.

14. Oswald Chambers, *My Utmost for His Highest* (1935; reprint, Uhrichsville, Ohio: Barbour, 1963), 9.

Chapter Four: Humility's Impostors

1. Oswald Chambers, *Devotions for a Deeper Life* (Grand Rapids: Zondervan, 1986), 30.

2. *Vine's Expository Dictionary of New Testament Words,* s.v. "phobos" (fear).

3. For more on the subject of centeredness, see chapter 5 in my book *How to Act Right When Your Spouse Acts Wrong* (Colorado Springs: WaterBrook, 2001).

4. John Bevere, *The Fear of the Lord: Discover the Key to Intimately Knowing God* (Orlando: Creation House, 1997), 71.

5. Calvin Miller, *Into the Depths of God* (Minneapolis: Bethany, 2000), 206.

6. François Fénelon, *Christian Perfection,* trans. Mildred Whitney Stillman (Minneapolis: Bethany, 1975), 186.

7. Miller, *Into the Depths of God,* 211.

8. Christina Rossetti, *Poems and Prose,* ed. Jan Marsh, (Boston: Tuttle, 1994), 84-5.

Chapter Five: Jesus: Our Example of Selflessness

1. Andrew Murray, *Humility* (Gainsville, Fla.: Bridge-Logos Publishers, 2000), 19.
2. Francis de Sales, *Introduction to the Devout Life* (New York: Doubleday, 1989), 127.

Chapter Six: The Fear of God Leads to Humility

1. Oswald Chambers, *My Utmost for His Highest* (1935; reprint, Uhrichsville, Ohio: Barbour, 1963), 31.
2. A. W. Tozer, *The Best of A. W. Tozer* (Grand Rapids: Baker, 1978), 218-9.
3. Henry Nouwen, *The Only Necessary Thing* (New York: Crossroad, 1999), 170.
4. John Bevere, *The Fear of the Lord: Discover the Key to Intimately Knowing God* (Orlando: Creation House, 1997), 26.
5. Tozer, *Best of A. W. Tozer,* 14.
6. Tozer, *Best of A. W. Tozer,* 23.
7. Oswald Chambers, *Biblical Psychology: Christ-Centered Solutions for Daily Problems* (Grand Rapids: Discovery House, 1995), 121.
8. Andrew Murray, *Humility* (Gainsville, Fla.: Bridge-Logos Publishers, 2000), 65.
9. My pastor, Howard Lawler, gave a series of sermons on the fear of the Lord, and he used this definition to summarize it.
10. Bevere, *The Fear of the Lord,* 21.
11. Murray, *Humility,* 68.

Chapter Seven: Are You a Fan or a Friend?

1. Howard Baker, *Soul Keeping: Ancient Paths of Spiritual Direction* (Colorado Springs: NavPress, 1998), 89.

2. C. S. Lewis, *Mere Christianity* (New York: MacMillan, 1969), 109.

3. Mark Buchanan, *Your God Is Too Safe* (Sisters, Oreg.: Multnomah, 2001), 205-6.

4. Larry Crabb, "Knowing God," in *The Soul Care Study Bible* (Nashville: Nelson, 2001), 164.

5. François Fénelon, *Christian Perfection,* trans. Mildred Whitney Stillman (Minneapolis: Bethany, 1975), 78.

6. *Vine's Expository Dictionary,* s.v. "metanoia."

7. John Bevere, *The Fear of the Lord: Discover the Key to Intimately Knowing God* (Orlando: Creation House, 1997), 100.

8. Andrew Murray, *Humility* (Gainsville, Fla.: Bridge-Logos Publishers, 2000), 4.

Chapter Eight: Growing in Selflessness

1. Andrew Murray, *Humility* (Gainsville, Fla.: Bridge-Logos Publishers, 2000), 3.

2. Gary Thomas, *Seeking the Face of God* (Nashville: Nelson, 1994), 126.

3. *Vine's Expository Dictionary,* s.v. "sanctification."

4. Gary Thomas, *The Glorious Pursuit: Embracing the Virtues of Christ* (Colorado Springs: NavPress, 1998), 49.

5. William Law, *A Serious Call to a Devout and Holy Life* (Grand Rapids: Baker, 1977), 180.

6. Law, *A Serious Call,* 181.

7. François Fénelon, *Christian Perfection,* trans. Mildred Whitney Stillman (Minneapolis: Bethany, 1975), 22-3.

8. Theresa of Avila, *Interior Castle* (New York: Doubleday, 1989), 38.

9. John Calvin quoted in John F. Bettler, "Gaining an Accurate Self-Image," *Journal of Biblical Counseling* 7, no. 3 (1984): 51.

10. Oswald Chambers, *My Utmost for His Highest* (1935; reprint, Uhrichsville, Ohio: Barbour, 1963), 251.

11. Calvin Miller, *The Unchained Soul* (Minneapolis: Bethany, 1998), xiii.

12. Thomas, *Seeking the Face of God,* 224.

13. François Fénelon, *Talking with God* (Brewster, Mass.: Paraclete Press, 1997), 115.

14. Thomas, *Seeking the Face of God,* 84.

15. Lauren White, "Humility, the Elusive Virtue," *Discipleship Journal,* no. 24 (1984): 32.

16. Richard J. Foster, *Celebration of Discipline: The Path to Spiritual Growth* (San Francisco: HarperSanFrancisco, 1998), 130.

17. Chambers, *My Utmost for His Highest,* 123.

18. François Fénelon, *Meditations and Devotions,* quoted in Bernard Bangley, *Near to the Heart of God* (Wheaton: Harold Shaw, 1998), November 9.

19. Foster, *Celebration of Discipline,* 130.

Chapter Nine: The Secret to Great Relationships

1. Dick Keyes, *Beyond Identity: Finding Your Self in the Image and Character of God* (Ann Arbor, Mich.: Servant, 1984), 97, quoted in Leanne Payne, *Restoring the Christian Soul* (Grand Rapids: Baker, 1991), 58.

2. Romano Guardini, quoted in Payne, *Restoring the Christian Soul,* 31.

3. John Piper, *Desiring God: Meditations of a Christian Hedonist* (Portland, Oreg.: Multnomah, 1986), 222.

4. Piper, *Desiring God,* 225.

5. Lloyd Ogilvie, *The Soul Care Study Bible* (Nashville: Nelson, 2001), 436.

6. Henry Scougal, *The Life of God in the Soul of Man* (Fearn, Scotland: Christian Heritage, 1996), 84.

7. François Fénelon, *Meditations on the Heart of God* (Brewster, Mass.: Paraclete Press, 1997), 61.

8. Thomas à Kempis, *Imitation of Christ* (Uhrichsville, Ohio: Barbour, 1984), 21.

9. For a more thorough understanding of this concept, see chapters 1 and 2 of my book *How to Act Right When Your Spouse Acts Wrong* (Colorado Springs: WaterBrook, 2001).

10. Mary O'Driscoll, ed., *Catherine of Siena, Selected Spiritual Writings* (New Rochelle, N.Y.: New City Press, 1993), 112.

11. Gary Thomas, *Seeking the Face of God* (Nashville: Nelson, 1994), 231.

12. Francis de Sales, *Introduction to the Devout Life* (New York: Doubleday, 1989), 148-9.

13. For more specifics on how to love biblically, see chapters 8 and 9 of my book *How to Act Right When Your Spouse Acts Wrong.*

14. Andrew Murray, *Humility* (Gainsville, Fla.: Bridge-Logos Publishers, 2000), 55.

Chapter Ten: The Joy of a Life Well Lived

1. Calvin Miller, *Into the Depths of God* (Minneapolis: Bethany, 2000), 172.

2. Oswald Chambers, *My Utmost for His Highest* (1935; reprint, Uhrichsville, Ohio: Barbour, 1963), 105.

3. Thomas à Kempis, *Imitation of Christ* (Uhrichsville, Ohio: Barbour, 1984), 74.

4. Bernard of Clairvaux, *On Loving God,* quoted in Bernard Bangley, *Near to the Heart of God* (Wheaton: Harold Shaw, 1998), January 23.

5. Oswald Chambers, *Devotions for a Deeper Life* (Grand Rapids: Zondervan, 1986), 47.

6. Miller, *Into the Depths of God,* 135.

7. *Merriam Webster's Collegiate Dictionary,* 10th ed., s.v. "hope."

8. Quoted in James Hefley and Marti Hefley, *By Their Blood: Christian Martyrs of the Twentieth Century* (Milford, Mich.: Mott Media, 1981), 24.

9. Kempis, *Imitation of Christ,* 12.

10. Arthur Bennett, ed., *The Valley of Vision: A Collection of Puritan Prayers and Devotions* (Carlisle, Penn.: Banner of Truth, 1975), 13.

Study and Discussion Guide

1. Charles Colson, *Loving God* (Grand Rapids: Zondervan, 1983), 13.

2. A. W. Tozer, *The Best of A. W. Tozer* (Grand Rapids: Baker, 1978), 30.

3. William Law, *A Serious Call to a Devout and Holy Life* (Grand Rapids: Baker, 1977), 174.

4. Francis de Sales, *Introduction to the Devout Life* (New York: Doubleday, 1989), 149.

5. Gary Thomas, *Seeking the Face of God* (Nashville: Nelson, 1994), 117.

6. Charles Haddon Spurgeon, *Morning and Evening* (Peabody, Mass.: Hendrickson, 1995), 7.

7. De Sales, *Introduction to the Devout Life*, 124.

About the Author

Leslie is a popular speaker at conferences, women's retreats, and couples' retreats. She loves to encourage and motivate people to deepen their relationship with God and others. If you would like to schedule Leslie for a retreat or conference, contact her at 1-877-837-7931, or visit her Web site at www.leslievernick.com.

To learn more about WaterBrook Press and view
our catalog of products, log on to our Web site:
www.waterbrookpress.com